Willard H Hinkley

The book of Daniel

Its prophetic character and spiritual meaning

Willard H Hinkley

The book of Daniel
Its prophetic character and spiritual meaning

ISBN/EAN: 9783337334239

Printed in Europe, USA, Canada, Australia, Japan

Cover: Foto ©Lupo / pixelio.de

More available books at **www.hansebooks.com**

The Book of Daniel

Its Prophetic Character and

Spiritual Meaning

BY

WILLARD H. HINKLEY,

Pastor of the Church of the New Jerusalem, Brookline, Mass.

BOSTON:
MASSACHUSETTS NEW-CHURCH UNION
16 Arlington Street
1894

EXPLANATION OF REFERENCES.

The References at the close of each Chapter of the Book of Daniel are to different works of Swedenborg in which the Chapters and Verses cited are either simply quoted by way of illustration or explained as to their spiritual meaning. As the following commentaries are based upon the teachings of Swedenborg, the References will be found of great value.

As the initials only of the English titles of the works referred to are used, a Table is here added of the Titles, somewhat abbreviated.

Exceptions are the Latin titles "Dicta Probantia" (Dict. P.), the "Coronis," and the "Adversaria" (Adver.).

All the references have been taken from the Index of Le Boys Des Guays.

TABLE.

A. C.   Arcana Cœlestia.
A. E.   Apocalypse Explained.
A. R.   Apocalypse Revealed.
T. C. R.   True Christian Religion.
H. & H.   Heaven and Hell.
L. J.   Last Judgment.
C. L. J.   Continuation of the Last Judgment.
D. L. & W.   Divine Love and Wisdom.
D. P.   Divine Providence.
D. Lord.   Doctrine concerning the Lord.
D. S. S.   Doctrine concerning the Sacred Scripture.
D. F.   Doctrine of Faith.
D. L.   Doctrine of Life.
C. L.   Conjugial Love.
B. E.   Brief Exposition of the Doctrine of the New Church.
P. P.   Internal sense of the Prophets and Psalms.

INTRODUCTION.

I.

GENERAL CHARACTER OF THE BOOK.

THE book called Daniel is one of the inspired books of the Word. Although doubts have been cast upon its Divine origin and authenticity, owing to some difficulties in its literal statements, yet we have sufficient authority for accepting it as a part of Divine Revelation, or the Word of God, not only because it was quoted by the Lord Himself, but from the fact that it is included in the list of books that constitute the Word, as given in the writings of the New Church.

In these writings portions of it are explained according to their spiritual meaning. The book itself is both historical and prophetical. In the work entitled "Arcana Cœlestia" (n. 1183), we find the "land of Shinar" mentioned, and we are there told that in that land profane worship prevailed — that is, such worship as was holy in externals but evil in internals. In this passage the second verse of the first chapter of Daniel is quoted, and the carrying away of the Jews into Babylon is referred to as an historical relation. The fact that they were carried there and held captive has, probably, never been disputed, but the date assigned to this event in connection with the name of the King of Judah, is thought by some commentators to be erroneous.

Although the different events recorded in the book are generally believed to have taken place about 600 B. C., yet the composition of a part, at least, of the book has been ascribed by some writers to a period as late as 176–164, B. C., in the reign of Antiochus Epiphanes. If we had certain evidence that the book was not written by Daniel himself, this would not destroy its spiritual value. All that is contained in the five books of Moses was not written by him, but they were written by some hand; partly by Moses and partly by some one after his death. This fact does not weaken their authority nor destroy their spiritual meaning.

The book called Daniel is not only twofold in character, historical and prophetical, but it is written in two languages, Hebrew and Aramaic. Chapter i. and chapters viii. to xii. are written in Hebrew, and from chapter ii. ver. 4 to the end of chapter vii. is written in Aramaic.

The book is usually divided according to these differences. But there seems to be no reason for such a division, so far as its spiritual meaning is concerned. It has been suggested that the whole book was originally written in Hebrew and afterwards in Aramaic, but that portions of the original Hebrew were lost, and that these were afterwards supplied from copies in Aramaic.

We do not regard these questions as unimportant, by any means, although a few only, even among Biblical scholars, can arrive at a final conclusion regarding them.

We are obliged to treat the Word as we now possess

it, believing that under the Divine Providence it has been preserved and handed down to us.

We should regard the book of Daniel as a whole, knowing that it was written for the sake of its spiritual meaning, and not for the purpose of recording historical events in a connected series. Wherever its statements and allusions seem to conflict with the facts of actual history, we may be sure that these apparent difficulties can be reconciled. Two instances of this kind may be mentioned. When Belshazzar is spoken of, he is called the son of Nebuchadnezzar; but it seems to have been satisfactorily shown that he was not the son but the grandson of that king.

In the spiritual sense, this apparent inaccuracy does not impair the meaning or change it. A grandson equally with a son denotes some derivative principle, here a false principle derived from evil. Similar instances of this use of the term son, and also of the term brother, may be found in the Word.

Another instance, more difficult to be reconciled, is the statement in regard to the transfer of the Babylonish empire. In chapter v. ver. 31, we read: "And Darius, the Mede, received the kingdom, being about three score and two years old." But in the history of those times gathered from ancient documents, it is related as a positive undoubted fact, that it was Cyrus who acquired the kingdom of Babylon. The only way to reconcile the difference is to suppose that this Darius of the book of Daniel was some prince to whom the power of governing Babylonia was delegated by Cyrus.

The book of Daniel does not contain a connected

history of natural events, but all the historical events mentioned have been recorded for the sake of their spiritual meaning. This may be said of all the historical parts of the Word, even of the Gospels.

In regard to the prophetic visions of Daniel, it is very plain, in the light of the explanations given in the writings of the New Church, that they can only be interpreted according to the law of correspondence and representation, and that no explanation can be satisfactory which makes reference only to a succession of empires, or to merely natural events.

Even when this book of Daniel is explained with reference to the state of the Christian church, especially of the Roman Catholic and Protestant branches, there is some danger of making the application too literal, making allusion to the outward condition of churches, rather than to principles of Divine truth and their operation, from which the internal quality of the church is made known. By a careful study of the book and of such explanations of it as are given in the writings of the New Church, we may see that principles, true or false, are always treated of, and outward changes or conditions are shown to be illustrations of the operation of these principles in the human mind and therefore in the church.

In studying the Word of the Lord in the light of true doctrine, we should rise above merely external things and endeavor to see its spiritual meaning, not only in relation to churches and dispensations, which is called the historical-spiritual sense, but in reference to individual states of life and especially to our own life.

What, then, is the spirit and purpose of this revelation, contained in the book of Daniel? What are the particulars contained in the spiritual sense of it? To know these things we must first have some idea of the general subjects treated of. There are three general subjects treated of in the whole book. These are "the Consummation, or last time of the Church," "the Coming of the Lord," and "the New Church," signified in the Apocalypse by the New Jerusalem. "Wherever Daniel is mentioned by name in the Sacred Scriptures, he represents whatever is prophetic concerning the Coming of the Lord — and the state of the church at the last times." (A. C. 3652.)

The captivity of the Jews in Babylon represents a state of the church and of the human mind in which man has fallen under the influence of the infernal love of dominion, the love of ruling over others originating in the love of self. Babylon always denotes that evil love, and to be in Babylon is to be under its influence.

So many allusions to Babylon and direct statements regarding it are found in the Sacred Scriptures, especially in the prophecy of Isaiah and in the book of Revelation, that no doubt can be entertained that this is its spiritual meaning. Indeed, from the first mention of Babylon in Genesis to the declarations in the Apocalypse with regard to "Babylon the Great, the mother of harlots and abominations of the earth," its representation is uniform. This has long been recognized by writers on the meaning of Scripture symbols. But only in the writings of the New Church do we find an explanation of the particulars involved or expressed, especially with reference to the different ages or dispensations. The Jewish Church finally came under the influence of this evil love to such a degree that it was brought to an end. This is denoted by the captivity of Israel and Judah.

This love of dominion existed with the priests and kings of that church long before its end. Its final consummation was represented by the taking of Jerusalem by Nebuchadnezzar, and the carrying of a number of its inhabitants into captivity, just as an individual loses power over himself and all freedom of action when he allows himself to be governed by this evil love, or is carried away by it, even for a time.

At the end of every church or dispensation, however, there are remains of good out of which a new church can be formed. The old must be utterly vastated or consummated before anything new can spring up. Indeed there must be a judgment upon the old. The evil love of ruling over others is allowed to extend itself to the utmost limit, that is, as far as it can go, until it is consummated by its own fury; then it is overthrown and a new life springs up. In all the past history of the human race there has been this extremity of evil, the growth of the lust of dominion, which continues until it produces insanity and destroys itself. This is plainly shown in what is said of Nebuchadnezzar and Belshazzar. But the remains of good (the "small remnant") although they may be obscured for a time, and become apparently lifeless, are continually sustained and kept alive by the Lord.

These remains are represented by Daniel and his

companions who are spoken of as certain of the children of Israel who are of the " King's seed." To be of the King's seed is to be in truths from the Lord.

The position and conduct of Daniel in Babylon is somewhat like that of Joseph in Egypt. In the highest sense, both of them represent the Lord.

The parallel between Daniel and the Lord may be seen somewhat from the life of the Lord as given in the Gospel. Regarding Daniel as representing the Lord as Divine Truth, we see that this truth has, at first, little or no power. It is apparently completely subject to the love of dominion exercised both spiritually and naturally, in Church and State. Nebuchadnezzar represents the love of dominion on the natural plane of life. There was no true church remaining in Babylonia; but the spiritual power was represented by the magicians, soothsayers, and astrologers.

The similarity of the book of Daniel to the book of Revelation called the Apocalypse, has been frequently alluded to. The visions of Daniel and John are of a similar character. The book of Daniel is apocalyptic. It is full of wonderful imagery, which clearly points to a future state of the church. Swedenborg says, in explanation of the Apocalypse, that "it does not treat of successive states of the church, still less of the successive states of kingdoms, as some have hitherto believed; but therein, from beginning to end, the last state of the church in the heavens and upon the earth, and then the Last Judgment, and after this a New Church which is the New Jerusalem." (A. R. 2.)

The same statement may be made with reference to

the book of Daniel. It is a book of the last times, showing the cause of the decline of every church and the loss of spiritual life in the individual man. Babylon, in the Apocalypse, is the Roman Catholic religion; in the book of Daniel it is the love of dominion, not only in the Roman Catholic Church, but in all churches from the beginning of the decline of the Most Ancient Church to the end of the First Christian Church. The second part of the three-fold subject, namely, the Coming of the Lord, is vividly portrayed in Daniel's own visions of the Lord as narrated in the seventh and tenth chapters.

In these chapters the prophetic character of the book, as relating to the Lord's Coming, is more plainly seen. To these visions we find much reference in the writings of the New Church.

This book has been little understood either in the Jewish Church or in the Christian Church. It could not be understood without a revelation of its spiritual meaning. Swedenborg has not given a connected relation of this spiritual meaning as he has of the Apocalypse. We must, therefore, make use of the explanations given of some portions of it, and rely upon a knowledge of the general law of interpretation to explain the rest.

In regard to the Apocryphal additions to the book of Daniel found in the Septuagint version, which are comprised under four books called: "The Prayer of Azarias," "The Song of the Three Children," "The History of Susanna," and "The Narrative of Bel and the Dragon," but little needs to be said. They are generally acknowledged to form no part of the original, but to have been constructed from it with fabulous and fanciful additions. Jerome, who translated them with the canonical parts of the book of Daniel from the Greek of Theodotion, declared that Daniel as received by the Hebrews contained neither of the last three named, and he probably included the " Prayer of Azarias."

II.

DANIEL THE PROPHET.

It is not well to dwell too much upon the personal character of the prophets. They simply represent the Lord as the great Prophet and Teacher. As representative men their private or personal character is not to be reflected upon, except so far as it serves to explain and illustrate the manifestation of the truth through them. In fact, we know but little about them — that is, nothing reliable beyond what is found in the letter of the Scriptures.

Daniel is not to be excepted from this rule of interpretation, although more is said of his personal life and experiences than of the other prophets. In the book called by his name, especially in its historical statements, the experiences of himself and other Hebrew young men who were with him in Babylon are narrated.

The additions to these statements, found in the Apocryphal books, are not worthy of credence. While, then, we must respect the principle of interpretation, above stated, we must recognize the fact that the natural life of such representative characters, their education, and, in some cases, their previous calling fitted and prepared them for their spiritual mission.

We know nothing definite of Daniel's parentage, but we have reason to believe that he sprang from a royal family, for Nebuchadnezzar, the king, commanded Ashpenaz, the master of the eunuchs, to carry with him to Babylon, of the children of Israel, some who were "of the seed royal" and of the "nobles," "youths in whom there was no blemish, but well favored and skilful in all wisdom, and cunning in knowledge and understanding science, and such as had ability to stand in the king's palace, and that he should teach them the learning and the tongue of the Chaldeans." (Chap. i. 3, 4.)

Josephus says that Daniel was the son of Zedekiah, the last King of Judah, whose name was changed from Mattaniah by Nebuchadnezzar, when he made him king instead of Jehoiachin. (See 2 KINGS xxiv. 17.) It is supposed by some that Daniel and his three companions were made eunuchs in the palace of the king, as Isaiah prophesied to King Hezekiah. (See 2 KINGS xx. 18: Is. xxxix. 7.) Of this, however, some doubt may be entertained. The Hebrew word *saris* has been translated, in some passages, *chamberlain* — an office which did not at a later day necessarily require a eunuch. The words of the prophecy would, however, if interpreted literally, sustain the supposition.

Daniel must have been prepared for his future office as a prophet of the Lord, first by his education and training in Jerusalem before he was carried into Babylon.

Nebuchadnezzar seems to have desired to make use of the knowledge possessed by the Jews for the glory of his kingdom, and to add to it the science and learning of the magicians, astrologers, and soothsayers of Chaldea, one of the former seats of the Ancient Church. In this way Daniel was prepared for receiving Divine truths and for becoming a chosen instrument for revealing hidden things by means of which the state of the church could be judged and known.

He did not understand the meaning of the revelations given to him in their relation to the internal or spiritual state of the church, but he could judge of the state of the world around him, and the worship of the Babylonians which was opposite to the worship of Jehovah. He set his face towards Jerusalem and prayed to the God of Israel, and not to the gods of the nations around him. The state of things around him in Nebuchadnezzar's kingdom was typical of the state of the church when the love of dominion, springing from the love of self, prevails over love to the Lord. At the same time he was enabled to describe the things shown to him in vision, which were antetypes of natural things and thus represented and signified the state of the church on earth. His very name has reference to the Divine judgment, for Daniel means, " God is Judge."

In his prophetic character, he not only represents what all the prophets do — that is, the truth itself which reveals and foretells the future state of the church — but in a special and peculiar manner he represents the Lord as a revealer of Divine truths by which human souls are liberated from the bondage of evil. Daniel was a light in a dark place, as Joseph was in Egypt. His life and experiences resemble those of Joseph in many ways. Carried into captivity, he learned submission in order that he might command. Amid luxury and vice he abstained from them, and was thus, like John the Baptist, a Nazarite — or one set apart and consecrated, by a vow, to stand before the Lord as well as before an earthly king in a pure and holy life. There is something sublime in his self-denial and renunciation of evil, which marks him in a peculiar manner as a representative of the Divine prophet, who was wiser than the sons of men, and "purer than snow and whiter than milk."

In the explanations given in the writings of the New Church of that portion of the twenty-fourth chapter of Matthew in which the prophecy of Daniel is alluded to, we read that "Daniel represents, when mentioned by name, whatsoever is prophetic concerning the coming of the Lord, and (in that chapter of Matthew especially) the state of the church at the last times." (A. C. 3652.) Again, it is there stated that the expression, "spoken of by Daniel the prophet, signifies in the internal sense, by the prophets; for where any prophet is mentioned by name in the Word, it does not mean that prophet, but the prophetic Word itself, because names in no case penetrate into heaven; nevertheless each prophet has a distinct signification." These teachings indicate that Daniel represents the Lord, especially as He manifests Himself at the end of the church, and in His coming to judgment, not only in His first coming, but in every appearing of the Son of Man when the darkness and desolation of the night are passing away, and the dawn is breaking.

It is well to note here that Swedenborg, in the printing of the work called "True Christian Religion," placed immediately after the title page, two passages from the Word to indicate the character of that work. The first of these passages is from the book of Daniel (chap. vii. 13, 14), which contains Daniel's vision of the Son of Man with the clouds of heaven ; the second is from the book of the Revelation of John where the New Heaven and the New Earth and the New Jerusalem are spoken of. This not only shows that the prophecy of Daniel treats of the Lord's coming, but it also connects it directly with the descent of the New Jerusalem. Thus Swedenborg indicated plainly what modern commentators have partially seen — the resemblance between Daniel's visions and those of John the Revelator. They are similar, not only because they treat of the same subjects, but because their vision was of a similar nature. The subjects principally treated of, in both of these books, is the "Consummation of the Age, or the Last Time of the Church," the "Coming of the Lord," and the "New Heaven and the New Church." This is explained in chapter xiv. of the "True Christian Religion," in which passages from these two prophetical books of the Word are extensively quoted.

What was the character of the visions of Daniel and John is fully explained in n. 157 of the "True Christian Religion." There we read :

Since by the spirit of man is meant his mind, therefore by "being in the spirit," which is sometimes said in the Word, is meant a state of the mind separate from the body ; and because in that state the prophets saw such things as exist in the spiritual world, therefore that is called the vision of God. Their state, then, was such as that of spirits themselves and angels in that world. In that state the spirit of man like his mind, as to sight, may be transported from place to place, the body remaining in its own. This is the state in which I have now been for twenty-six years, with this difference, that I have been in the spirit and at the same time in the body, and only sometimes out of the body. That Ezekiel, Zechariah, Daniel, and John when he wrote the Revelation, were in that state is evident from the following passages.

Quotations are then given from these prophets and from John.

There can be no doubt that Daniel before he was carried into captivity had been educated in the law of Moses and in a knowledge of Jehovah. He obeyed and worshipped the God of Israel when he was in Babylon, rather than the false gods around him. He had strength to resist the seductive influences of the royal court of Babylon, because of his previous education and training at Jerusalem. He was in the king's house, but did not eat of the king's meat. Thus must every child of God who would become gifted with a knowledge of heavenly and Divine things, be prepared by abstinence from the indulgence of selfish and worldly loves for spiritual illumination. But Daniel was not only prepared by his education in Jerusalem, but by instruction in the knowledge of ancient things, or in the learning of the Chaldeans, in the palace of the king and by his direction. Thus he was like Moses, who was "learned in all the wisdom of the Egyptians." (Acts vii. 22.) We may believe that he received from the Magi, or wise men of that country, a knowledge of natural science, so far as it was known at that day, and especially of the correspondence of earthly things with heavenly. He was thus prepared for his holy office, for the opening of his spiritual sight, and for his actual intromission into the spiritual world. In the passage already quoted from the "True Christian Religion" (n. 157), the nature of his vision is plainly taught. It was not simply a mental state due to natural causes, but an actual opening of his spiritual senses so that he was present with angels and spirits in the spiritual world.

It may be thought from its being said that an angel spoke to him, and especially that Michael helped him and Gabriel spoke to him (chap. viii. 16; ix. 21; x. 13), that he was instructed as to the spiritual meaning of his visions by an individual angel. But we are informed in the work concerning "Heaven and its Wonders and concerning Hell," that Michael, Gabriel, and Raphael are only angelic societies which are so named from their functions. (No. 52.)

Are we not to understand therefore, that while Daniel, Ezekiel, Zechariah, and others had visions of angels, one or more appearing to them, that they were brought into actual communication with one or more heavenly societies, so that they received by influx some knowledge from these societies in regard to the Lord and His love and what He was about to do for human redemption, the individual angels serving only as representatives or messengers. The prophets were not instructed as to the spiritual meaning of these heavenly communications. Each heavenly society has its own peculiar function. The function of the society denoted in the Word by Gabriel must have reference to the Lord's coming to judgment. It was Gabriel who announced the Lord's birth to the Virgin Mary. This view may be fully confirmed by reference to the work entitled "The Apocalypse Revealed" (n. 548), where we are taught that by Michael is meant the ministry of those who prove from the Word that the Lord is the God of heaven and earth, and that God the Father and He are one, as the soul and body are one, also that man must live according to the precepts of the Decalogue, and that he then has charity and faith; and that "by Gabriel is meant the ministry of those who teach from the Word that Jehovah came into the world, and that the human which He there begat is the Son of God and Divine."

From these things adduced from the writings of Swedenborg, the Servant of the Lord, in making known His Second Coming, something may be understood of the prophetic character of Daniel.

CHAPTER I.

In the third year of the reign of Jehoiakim king of Judah came Nebuchadnezzar king of Babylon unto Jerusalem, and 2 besieged it. And the Lord gave Jehoiakim king of Judah into his hand, with part of the vessels of the house of God; and he carried them into the land of Shinar to the house of his god: and he brought the vessels into the treasure house 3 of his god. And the king spake unto Ashpenaz the master of his eunuchs, that he should bring in *certain* of the children 4 of Israel, even of the seed royal and of the nobles; youths in whom was no blemish, but well favoured, and skilful in all wisdom, and cunning in knowledge, and understanding science, and such as had ability to stand in the king's palace; and that he should teach them the learning and the tongue 5 of the Chaldeans. And the king appointed for them a daily portion of the king's meat, and of the wine which he drank, and that they should be nourished three years; that at the 6 end thereof they might stand before the king. Now among these were, of the children of Judah, Daniel, Hananiah, 7 Mishael, and Azariah. And the prince of the eunuchs gave names unto them; unto Daniel he gave *the name of* Belteshazzar; and to Hananiah, *of* Shadrach; and to Mishael, *of* 8 Meshach; and to Azariah, *of* Abednego. But Daniel purposed in his heart that he would not defile himself with the king's meat, nor with the wine which he drank; therefore he requested of the prince of the eunuchs that he might not 9 defile himself. Now God made Daniel to find favour and 10 compassion in the sight of the prince of the eunuchs. And the prince of the eunuchs said unto Daniel, I fear my lord the king, who hath appointed your meat and your drink: for why should he see your faces worse liking than the youths 11 which are of your own age? so should ye endanger my head with the king. Then said Daniel to the steward, whom the prince of the eunuchs had appointed over Daniel, Hananiah, 12 Mishael, and Azariah: Prove thy servants, I beseech thee, ten days; and let them give us pulse to eat, and water to 13 drink. Then let our countenances be looked upon before thee, and the countenance of the youths that eat of the 14 king's meat; and as thou seest, deal with thy servants. So he hearkened unto them in this matter, and proved them 15 ten days. And at the end of ten days their countenances appeared fairer, and they were fatter in flesh, than all the 16 youths which did eat of the king's meat. So the steward took away their meat, and the wine that they should drink, 17 and gave them pulse. Now as for these four youths, God gave them knowledge and skill in all learning and wisdom: and Daniel had understanding in all visions and dreams. 18 And at the end of the days which the king had appointed for bringing them in, the prince of the eunuchs brought 19 them in before Nebuchadnezzar. And the king communed with them; and among them all was found none like Daniel, Hananiah, Mishael, and Azariah: therefore stood they be- 20 fore the king. And in every matter of wisdom and understanding, concerning which the king inquired of them, he found them ten times better than all the magicians and en- 21 chanters that were in all his realm. And Daniel continued even unto the first year of King Cyrus.

REFERENCES.

Verses.								Numbers.
1, 2	.	.	.	.	.	.	.	P. P.
2	.	.	.	.	.	.	.	A. C. 1183
3–21	.	.	.	.	.	.	.	P. P.
19, 20	.	.	.	.	A. C. 5223;	A. E. 675
20	.	.	.	.	.	.	.	A. R. 101

COMMENTARY.

DANIEL IN BABYLON.

THE carrying away of the Jews into Babylon, by Nebuchadnezzar, in the reign of Jehoiakim, King of Judah, is an historical fact. There seems to be some doubt, however, as to the precise date of the event. The opening verse of chapter one of this book is in these words:

In the third year of the reign of Jehoiakim King of Judah came Nebuchadnezzar King of Babylon unto Jerusalem, and besieged it.

In the prophecy of JEREMIAH, xxxvi. 1, we read:

And it came to pass in the fourth year of Jehoiakim, the son of Josiah, King of Judah, this word came unto Jeremiah from the Lord.

Then follows the prophecy which was read before the king and so angered him that he burnt up the roll on which it was written, piecemeal, in the fire by which he was warming himself in his winter palace.

Dr. William Smith, remarking on the apparent difficulty in the dates, says:

The simplest explanation is, that the advance of Nebuchadnezzar from Babylon began in the third year of Jehoiakim, but that Jerusalem was not taken until the fourth.

We would emphasize the doctrine of the New Church familiar to our readers, that the Word of the Lord, as given in history and prophecy, was written solely for the sake of its spiritual meaning. We need not be troubled, therefore, concerning any apparent difficulties in its literal statements. The "third year" denotes a state of fulness; here it denotes a state in which evil had come to the full, when there was a complete vastation of the church. Its worship became profane and idolatrous, and it fell under the dominion of the love of ruling from the love of self.

It may be well, however, to refer to some of the historical facts connected with the story of the captivity, as they now seem to have been established. Jehoiakim, whose original name was Eliakim, was set up to be King of Judah, by Necho, King of Egypt.

After the battle of Carchemish, near the Euphrates, when the Egyptians were defeated by the Babylonians, Jerusalem was besieged and captured by Nebuchadnezzar. He first took Jehoiakim prisoner, but afterwards suffered him to remain in Jerusalem as a vassal king, tributary to the Babylonian power. After three years, Jehoiakim rebelled against Nebuchadnezzar. Jerusalem was then again attacked, not by Nebuchadnezzar in person, but by numerous bands of Syrians, Moabites, and Ammonites, who were then subject to the King of Babylon. Jehoiakim was killed, his body was cast out, and afterwards buried in an ignominious manner beyond the gates of Jerusalem, as prophesied by Jeremiah.

Sometime afterwards Jehoiachin, the son of Jehoiakim, sometimes called Jechoniah, reigned for three months. But there was again a rebellious spirit manifested, and Jehoiachin was taken prisoner, carried into Babylon, and held there in close captivity for thirty-six years. A large number of captives — among them Daniel and his royal companions — were carried away at the first capture of Jerusalem, and another portion, said to number ten thousand, were taken into captivity with Jehoiachin. (2 KINGS xxiv. 14.)

The fact is now established that Nebuchadnezzar was coregent with his father Nabopolasser, in the latter part of his father's reign and that he was called king by anticipation. At the time of the battle of Carchemish and the first siege of Jerusalem, he was not sole and absolute King of Babylon. The time of Daniel's probation, according to chapter one, verse five, was three years, but it was in the second year of the king's actual reign that he was brought before him to interpret his dream.

These things will not be regarded, however, as of primary importance if we believe that the literal narrative is simply a vehicle for communicating the spiritual meaning, which relates not to the rise and fall of kingdoms, but to the state of the church and of the human mind in which the church is established.

The spiritual sense of the Word is threefold. In its highest or inmost sense it treats of the Lord and the glorification of His humanity, in the next lower sense it reveals the laws and processes of man's regeneration, and in its lowest sense — called the historical-spiritual sense — it treats of the different states of the church. The prophecy of Daniel relates more particularly to the consummation of the church and the coming of the Lord to judgment.

Jehoiakim, it is plain from Jeremiah, was a profane and idolatrous king. He represents, therefore, the evil love of dominion in the church, which leads to profanation. What then is represented by Nebuchadnezzar? Both were kings, and both sought dominion. The kingdom of Judah was a theocracy. The civil power and the ecclesiastical power were united, and Jehovah alone was the head of the church. Nevertheless, there was a priesthood and a sovereignty. When these became perverted the whole church was perverted.

The nations and peoples outside of Canaan represented the natural or external principles of human life and the natural degree of the mind. When this plane of the mind is altogether separated from what is spiritual, the natural love of dominion seeks preëminence. This is destructive of the church and of all genuine religion. Nebuchadnezzar represents this natural evil love which seeks to make all things subservient to it.

In A. C. 10227, we read:

By Nebuchadnezzar, King of Babel, is meant the profane that vastates, which is the case when the truths and goods of the church serve for means to favor the evils of the love of self and of the world, by wrong application, for in such case the evils of those loves are inwardly in the heart, and the holy things of the church are in the mouth.

When the love of self takes the place of love to the Lord within the church, then the church falls a prey to the natural love of dominion, exercised on the natural plane of life, and all things are made subservient to it. Nebuchadnezzar was a waster and destroyer. It was predicted by Jeremiah that all who remained in Jerusalem would be destroyed by him. (Chap. xxxi.)

Now by the King of Babylon coming against Jerusalem, is meant that the church comes under the dominion of this natural evil love, and those within the church who have profaned holy things will lose all spiritual freedom. This is the spiritual meaning of Jeremiah's prediction.

But the church may continue to exist, externally, with all its outward forms of worship, after it has lost its spirituality and has come under the evil love of dominion. The captivity in Babylon is the bondage of the man of the church to this natural evil love of dominion, which usurps the place of love to the Lord. The individual who exercises it claims the worship which belongs to the Lord alone. The profanation of holy things is represented by the carrying away of the sacred vessels out of the temple by Nebuchadnezzar, and their being used at Belshazzar's feast by the revellers.

In order to have a general idea of the spiritual meaning of this book called Daniel, we must think, in the first place, of the state of the Jewish Church as depicted by Isaiah, Jeremiah, and Ezekiel. The Jewish Church had already profaned and adulterated holy things. The first conquest of the kingdom of Israel, and the captivity of its people by the Assyrians, denotes the perversion of the intellectual principle of the mind and its subjection to false reasonings, while the conquest of the kingdom of Judah, and the captivity of its people in Babylon, denotes the subjection of the will principle to the infernal love of dominion.

The Jewish Church, at the period of the second captivity, was vastated. If it had not been Nebuchadnezzar could not so easily have led the men of Judah into captivity, after destroying so many of the inhabitants of

Jerusalem. But while the church in its external form may be destroyed, when men cease to love and obey its holy truths, yet these truths themselves can never be wholly extinguished. Even after the church has fallen under the dominion of the love of self, some truths remain in the minds of a few. There is a "small remnant" by which the human race can be saved from utter extinction.

Daniel and the other children of the King's seed, "well-favored and in whom there was no blemish," represent the truths of the church which remain, and serve as new seed from which faith in the Lord may be born anew.

The gift of prophecy was not entirely lost even after the Jewish Church became corrupt. The prophets condemned the evils around them — Isaiah and Jeremiah in Jerusalem, and Ezekiel and Daniel in Babylon — and they suffered much, thus representing how the holy truths of the church and the Lord Himself suffered at the hands of evil men.

Daniel and his companions represent those who are in states of innocence, with whom the truth is preserved in dark and evil states of the church and amid much persecution. They would not eat of the king's meat in Babylon, some of which, doubtless, was offered to idols.

Nebuchadnezzar's command to his eunuch, or chamberlain, to bring these children of Judah into his palace that they might be taught the learning and tongue of the Chaldeans, denotes the will and purpose of those who are in the love of dominion from the love of self to make the truths of the church and all its holy principles subservient to their own selfish ends.

In the historical-spiritual sense, the particulars related in this chapter have reference to the state of the Jewish Church at its end, especially at the time of the Lord's coming, when its consummation was complete. They also refer to the state of the Christian Church at its end, especially when the Church of Rome attempted to bring the whole world under its dominion. The Roman Catholic religion is denoted by Babylon, but wherever the infernal love of dominion prevails there is Babylon. At the end of every church the natural selfish love of ruling over others prevails. Its object is worldly gain or power. The devil offered the Lord all the kingdoms of this world, and the glory of them, if He would fall down and worship him, but the Lord answered him: "Thou shalt worship the Lord thy God and Him only shalt thou serve."

The Roman Church has distinguished itself by efforts to obtain civil power for the sake of maintaining its own supremacy. But this end can no longer be secured, since "Babylon has fallen." Since the Last Judgment this power has been fully overcome in the spiritual world, so that neither the Roman Church, nor any other, can henceforth obtain power over the souls of men, or deprive them of spiritual freedom. The church will not rule over the State, nor will the State rule over the church, but each will perform its own use in the world and fill its own proper sphere.

As to Daniel he not only represents the truth remaining at the end of the Church, but, in the highest sense, he represents the Lord Himself as Divine Truth coming to judge the state of the church.

His conduct in refusing the king's meat and feeding on pulse, beautifully shows forth the nature of spiritual abstinence from natural evil delights which would destroy all remains of good in the soul.

The Lord, while He was tempted as to all the evils to which humanity was subject, resisted and overcame all these evils of every degree, and thus accomplished the work of redemption from the evil power.

He fulfilled the law of the Nazarite, not naturally — for He "came eating and drinking" — but spiritually, that is in a perfectly pure and holy life. He was a Nazarite, indeed, "purer than snow and whiter than milk."

In all matters of wisdom and understanding Daniel and his three companions were found to be ten times better than all the magicians and astrologers in the kingdom.

This was when they were brought before the king at the end of their probation. When the Lord stood in the temple before the doctors, He was found to possess wisdom much greater than theirs. Wherever the Divine Truth begins to gain a permanent influence in the human mind, it will be found to be higher than all the reasonings of the natural man. Daniel raised to power in Babylon represents the supremacy of Divine truth, and his three companions represent all inferior and subordinate truths of different degrees.

As Nebuchadnezzar became acquainted with Daniel, and learned what wisdom he possessed, he decided to make use of it to increase his own power. He found that it gave him more power than all the knowledge of the magicians and astrologers. Truths of a spiritual nature give greater power for evil as well as for good, but they are finally taken away from those who do not make good use of them.

In the last verse of this chapter it is written: "And Daniel continued even unto the first year of King Cyrus"; and in the twenty-eighth verse of the sixth chapter, we find these words: "So this Daniel prospered in the reign of Darius, and in the reign of Cyrus, the Persian." It was Cyrus, King of Persia, the real conquerer of Babylon, who assisted the Jewish people to return to their own land, and to rebuild the temple at Jerusalem, restoring to them the vessels of gold and silver that had not been destroyed.

We are told in A. C. 8989 that "Cyrus represents the Lord as to the Humanity."

The life of Daniel in Babylon, with the other captive Jews, represents the state of the church at its consummation, when the truth is held in subjection to the power of evil and remains only with a few; but the beginning of the reign of Cyrus denotes the coming of the Lord, first to restore natural freedom and then to establish a New Church in which the truth will be all powerful to overcome the dominion of evil, and whose members will acknowledge the Lord in His Divine Humanity and worship Him alone.

CHAPTER II.

And in the second year of the reign of Nebuchadnezzar Nebuchadnezzar dreamed dreams; and his spirit was
2 troubled, and his sleep brake from him. Then the king commanded to call the magicians, and the enchanters, and the sorcerers, and the Chaldeans, for to tell the king his
3 dreams. So they came in and stood before the king. And the king said unto them, I have dreamed a dream, and my
4 spirit is troubled to know the dream. Then spake the Chaldeans to the king in the Syrian language, O king, live for ever: tell thy servants the dream, and we will shew the
5 interpretation. The king answered and said to the Chaldeans, The thing is gone from me: if ye make not known unto me the dream and the interpretation thereof, ye shall be cut in pieces, and your houses shall be made a dunghill.
6 But if ye shew the dream and the interpretation thereof, ye shall receive of me gifts and rewards and great honour: therefore shew me the dream and the interpretation thereof.
7 They answered the second time and said, Let the king tell his servants the dream, and we will shew the interpretation.
8 The king answered and said, I know of a certainty that ye would gain time, because ye see the thing is gone from me.
9 But if ye make not known unto me the dream, there is but one law for you: for ye have prepared lying and corrupt words to speak before me, till the time be changed: therefore tell me the dream, and I shall know that ye can shew
10 me the interpretation thereof. The Chaldeans answered before the king, and said, There is not a man upon the earth that can shew the king's matter: forasmuch as no king, lord, nor ruler, hath asked such a thing of any magician or en-
11 chanter, or Chaldean. And it is a rare thing that the king requireth, and there is none other that can shew it before

the king, except the gods, whose dwelling is not with flesh.
12 For this cause the king was angry and very furious, and
13 commanded to destroy all the wise men of Babylon. So the decree went forth, and the wise men were to be slain; and
14 they sought Daniel and his companions to be slain. Then Daniel returned answer with counsel and prudence to Arioch the captain of the king's guard, which was gone forth
15 to slay the wise men of Babylon; he answered and said to Arioch the king's captain, Wherefore is the decree so urgent from the king? Then Arioch made the thing known to Dan-
16 iel. And Daniel went in, and desired of the king that he would appoint him a time, and he would shew the king the interpretation.
17 Then Daniel went to his house, and made the thing known to Hananiah, Mishael, and Azariah, his companions:
18 that they would desire mercies of the God of heaven concerning this secret; that Daniel and his companions should
19 not perish with the rest of the wise men of Babylon. Then was the secret revealed unto Daniel in a vision of the night.
20 Then Daniel blessed the God of heaven. Daniel answered and said, Blessed be the name of God for ever and ever: for wisdom and might are his: and he changeth the times and
21 the seasons: he removeth kings, and setteth up kings: he giveth wisdom unto the wise, and knowledge to them that
22 know understanding: he revealeth the deep and secret things: he knoweth what is in the darkness, and the light
23 dwelleth with him. I thank thee, and praise thee, O thou God of my fathers, who hast given me wisdom and might, and hast now made known unto me what we desired of thee:
24 for thou hast made known unto us the king's matter. Therefore Daniel went in unto Arioch, whom the king had appointed to destroy the wise men of Babylon: he went and said thus unto him; Destroy not the wise men of Babylon:

bring me in before the king, and I will shew unto the king the interpretation.

25 Then Arioch brought in Daniel before the king in haste, and said thus unto him, I have found a man of the children of the captivity of Judah, that will make known unto the king
26 the interpretation. The king answered and said to Daniel, whose name was Belteshazzar, Art thou able to make known unto me the dream which I have seen, and the interpreta-
27 tion thereof? Daniel answered before the king, and said, The secret which the king hath demanded can neither wise men, enchanters, magicians, nor soothsayers, shew unto the
28 king; but there is a God in heaven that revealeth secrets, and he hath made known to the king Nebuchadnezzar what shall be in the latter days. Thy dream, and the visions of
29 thy head upon thy bed, are these: as for thee, O king, thy thoughts came *into thy mind* upon thy bed, what should come to pass hereafter: and he that revealeth secrets hath
30 made known to thee what shall come to pass. But as for me, this secret is not revealed to me for any wisdom that I have more than any living, but to the intent that the interpretation may be made known to the king, and that thou
31 mayest know the thoughts of thy heart. Thou, O king, sawest, and behold a great image. This image, which was mighty, and whose brightness was excellent, stood before
32 thee; and the aspect thereof was terrible. As for this image, his head was of fine gold, his breast and his arms of
33 silver, his belly and his thighs of brass, his legs of iron, his
34 feet part of iron, and part of clay. Thou sawest till that a stone was cut out without hands, which smote the image upon his feet that were of iron and clay, and brake them in
35 pieces. Then was the iron, the clay, the brass, the silver, and the gold, broken in pieces together, and became like the chaff of the summer threshing floors; and the wind

carried them away, that no place was found for them: and the stone that smote the image became a great mountain, 36 and filled the whole earth. This is the dream; and we will 37 tell the interpretation thereof before the king. Thou, O king, art king of kings, unto whom the God of heaven hath given the kingdom, the power, and the strength, and the 38 glory; and wheresoever the children of men dwell, the beasts of the field and the fowls of the heaven hath he given into thine hand, and hath made thee to rule over them all: 39 thou art the head of gold. And after thee shall arise another kingdom inferior to thee; and another third kingdom 40 of brass, which shall bear rule over all the earth. And the fourth kingdom shall be strong as iron: forasmuch as iron breaketh in pieces and subdueth all things: and as iron that 41 crusheth all these, shall it break in pieces and crush. And whereas thou sawest the feet and toes, part of potters' clay, and part of iron, it shall be a divided kingdom; but there shall be in it of the strength of the iron, forasmuch as thou 42 sawest the iron mixed with miry clay. And as the toes of the feet were part of iron, and part of clay, so the kingdom 43 shall be partly strong, and partly broken. And whereas thou sawest the iron mixed with miry clay, they shall mingle themselves with the seed of men; but they shall not cleave one to another, even as iron doth not mingle with clay. 44 And in the days of those kings shall the God of heaven set up a kingdom, which shall never be destroyed, nor shall the sovereignty thereof be left to another people; but it shall break in pieces and consume all these kingdoms, and it 45 shall stand for ever. Forasmuch as thou sawest that a stone was cut out of the mountain without hands, and that it brake in pieces the iron, the brass, the clay, the silver, and the gold; the great God hath made known to the king what shall come to pass hereafter: and the dream is certain, and

46 the interpretation thereof sure. Then the king Nebuchadnezzar fell upon his face, and worshipped Daniel, and commanded that they should offer an oblation and sweet odours
47 unto him. The king answered unto Daniel, and said, Of a truth your God is the God of gods, and the Lord of kings, and a revealer of secrets, seeing thou hast been able to reveal
48 this secret. Then the king made Daniel great, and gave him many great gifts, and made him to rule over the whole province of Babylon, and to be chief governor over
49 all the wise men of Babylon. And Daniel requested of the king, and he appointed Shadrach, Meshach, and Abednego, over the affairs of the province of Babylon: but Daniel was in the gate of the king.

REFERENCES.

Verses.	Numbers.
1, 2	P. P.
3	D. Lord 48; T. C. R. 156
3–11	P. P.
12, 13	P. P.
14–30	P. P.
19, 20	A. C. 1422
22	A. C. 3384; A. E. 662
27	A. C. 3762
28	D. Lord 4; Dict. P. 11
31–33	A. C. 1837
31–35	D. S. S. 117; T. C. R. 275; A. E. 1029; P. P.
31–47	A. R. 717; T. C. R. 754
31–35, 44	Coronis 2
31, 32, 44, 45	A. C. 1326
32	A. R. 538; Coronis 37
32, 33	A. C. 1551, 2162, 3021, 10030, 10050; D. P. 328; A. R. 211, 775, 913; C. L. 78; A. E. 70, 577; Dict. P. 11
32–34, 41–43	A. E. 176

32, 33, 43	A. C. 9406
33, 40	A. C. 426
34, 35	A. C. 1298, 10030; A. E. 411
34-43	Dict. P. 11
34, 35, 44, 45	A. C. 6426, 8581; Dict. P. 11
35	T. C. R. 788
36-38	P. P.
37, 38	A. C. 1361; A. R. 567; A. E. 650, 1029
37-46	A. C. 2547
38	A. E. 1029
39	P. P.
40-43	P. P.
43	A. C. 10033, 10355; A. R. 781, 913; C. L. 73, 79; T. C. R. 761; A. E. 237, 411, 1029
43, 44	C. L. 81; T. C. R. 625
44	D. Lord 42; A. R. 664; T. C. R. 788; A. E. 411, 1029
44, 45	P. P.
45	A. R. 913
46-49	P. P.
47	A. C. 7401; A. R. 664
48	A. E. 844
Chapter cited	T. C. R. 760

COMMENTARY.

NEBUCHADNEZZAR'S DREAM OF THE GREAT IMAGE.

NEARLY the whole of the second chapter of Daniel is filled with an account of Nebuchadnezzar's dream of the great image and the interpretation of it by Daniel.

Dreams are commonly thought of, at this day, as something unreal, having no meaning. Such was not the case with the dreams of Nebuchadnezzar. In those days, and for a long period afterwards, revelations or communications from heaven were made by means of dreams. This may be seen from the Old Testament and from the New. It is a little remarkable that Nebuchadnezzar was not able to recall his dream of the great image, although he must have had an impression that it was of consequence to him. He had more than one dream, and the impressions they produced upon his mind induced anxiety and fear. They troubled him.

In the spiritual sense of the Word this dream denotes the revelation of Divine Truth. The particulars of the dream relate to the state of the church. This is especially seen in the interpretation given by Daniel. The state of the church, especially with respect to its consummation and the second coming of the Lord, could not have been known without a revelation from the Lord.

The nature of Divine revelation, even as to its form and manifestation, and especially as to its spiritual meaning, is such that it cannot be understood except by those who are enlightened by the Lord in a state of obedience, and who are in the desire of being led by the Lord. Those who are under the influence of the love of dominion cannot know the nature of Divine revelation ; they regard the Word of the Lord in the same light as they do any human production, and they endeavor to interpret it to suit their own evil desires.

Nebuchadnezzar preëminently represents those who are in this evil love of dominion. His kingdom was Babylon, which always denotes the rule or government of this evil love in the human mind ; that is, it denotes the church and the human mind entirely subject to the love of ruling over others from the love of self. There is, however, a good love of dominion and, in one sense, even Nebuchadnezzar represents this love, as we shall presently show.

When Nebuchadnezzar found that he could not remember his dream — it was gone from him — he called to him the magicians, the astrologers, the sorcerers, and the Chaldeans. It is not fully understood, at this day, what these several classes of men were, but enough is known to give us a general idea about them. We find them and their arts spoken of in the writings of the New Church. The magicians of Chaldea like those of Egypt were enabled by means of a knowledge of correspondences to induce a belief in the reality of certain things which were in fact unreal. They captivated the senses, charming and deceiving. In this way we are told they perverted correspondences and obtained power over the minds of others by objective means.

The astrologers were probably a distinct class from the magicians. They devoted themselves to the study of the heavenly bodies, and attributed to them or some of them certain attributes and powers and even worshipped them. They read in the stars the signs of future events and conditions of life. The sorcerers were another distinct class who acted directly upon the mind, producing a kind of mental stupor so as to keep one under their influence. In A. R. 462, there are three kinds of sorcery spoken of as follows:

Sorceries were in use among the ancients and were performed in three ways: first, by keeping the hearing and thus the mind of another continually intent upon his words and sayings, without retaining aught from them; and, at the same time, by an aspiration and inspiration of thought conjoined with affection, by means of the breath, into the sound of the voice, whereby the hearer is incapable of thinking anything from himself; in this manner did the lovers of falsehood pour in their falsities with violence. Secondly, they infused a persuasion, which was done by detaining the mind from everything of a contrary nature, and directing the attention exclusively to the idea involved in that which was uttered by themselves, hence the spiritual sphere of his mind dispelled the spiritual sphere of the mind of another, and stifled it; this was the kind of spiritual fascination which the magi of old made use of, and which was spoken of as the tying up and binding the understanding. The latter kind of sorcery pertained only to the spirit or thought but the former to the lips or speech also. Thirdly, the *hearer* kept his mind so fixed in his own opinion, that he almost shut his ears against hearing anything from the speaker, which was done by holding the breath and sometimes by a tacit muttering and thus by a continual negation of his adversary's sentiment. This kind of sorcery was practised by those who heard others, but the two former by those who spake to others.

These three kinds of sorcery prevailed among the ancients, and prevail still among infernal spirits; but with men in the world there remains only the third kind, and this with those, who, from the pride of their own intelligence, have confirmed in themselves the falsities of religion.

As to the word "Chaldeans," the term was probably applied at one time in a general way to all the inhabitants of Chaldea, but here it seems to denote a learned class who were known as such and who formed colleges for the cultivation of learning. Swedenborg not only says that the Chaldeans possessed a knowledge of correspondences but that they were acquainted with the internal sense of the Word. (A. C. 9011.) Whether they retained this knowledge at the time of Nebuchadnezzar is doubtful. But it is sufficient for us to know that neither they with all their learning, nor the magicians, astrologers, and sorcerers were able to read in the memory of the king the dream he had.

All these four classes of men represent those who pervert and profane the truth for their own selfish ends. Had they been permitted they would have interpreted the dream in such a way as to flatter and deceive the king, and thus confirm their own power. There are those even at the present day, who, although they deny the Divine in their hearts, are yet willing to use the Word for their own evil ends, and thus to falsify and profane it. Indeed, we must understand that every one who is in self-love and from this principle desires to gain power, either natural or spiritual, necessarily falsifies the truths of the Word when they are known to him. But many are kept in ignorance of the Word to prevent them from doing this. That all those upon whom the King of Babylon depended failed him, shows us that no one can from himself enter into a knowledge of Divine revelation or interpret the heavenly meaning of what the Lord has revealed. Daniel was able to do this because he was in illustration from the Lord. "The secret was revealed to Daniel in a night vision." He said to the king: "But as for me, this secret is not revealed to me for any wisdom that I have more than any living, but to the intent that the interpretation may be made known to the king, and that thou mightest know the thoughts of thy heart." (Chap. ii. ver. 30.)

The image was described by Daniel: "This image's head was of fine gold, his breast and his arms of silver, his belly and his thighs of brass, his legs of iron, his feet part of iron and part of clay."

In the "Coronis," no. 2, we are told that " four churches have existed on this earth since the creation of the world, the Adamic, the Noahtic, the Israelitish, and the Christian, which manifestly appears in Daniel, first by the statue seen by Nebuchadnezzar in a dream, and afterwards from the four beasts rising up out of the sea."

The common method of interpretation which finds in the four parts of the statue a reference to four earthly or political kingdoms, generally believed to be the Babylonian, the Medo-Persian, the Greek, and the Roman, is wholly inadequate for conveying the spiritual meaning, as may be seen from this little work called the "Coronis." This traditional interpretation is naturally drawn from the interpretation of the dream given by Daniel, understood only according to the letter.

In A. R. 913, which is referred to in the "Coronis," and more fully in A. C. 10,030, we find a particular explanation of the meaning of the parts of the great image. It is to be understood that this great image represents the successive states of the church. We are not to confine the interpretation to the four churches above named, as represented by the gold, the silver, the brass, and the iron. Each one of these four churches or dispensations has had its different changes corresponding to the different parts of the image. In "Coronis" no. 5 we read: "There have been four successive states or periods of every one of the above-named churches." Much confusion about the meaning of the Book of Daniel has arisen from ignorance of the true method of spiritual interpretation, and from attempting to apply the prophecy almost wholly to the Roman Catholic Church. That Babel or Babylon refers to this church or its religion, especially in the seventeenth chapter of the Apocalypse, is plainly taught in the writings of the New Church. But this great image represents all the states of the church down to the period of the Last Judgment and the Second Coming of the Lord. This last period is denoted by these words: "And whereas thou sawest iron mixed with miry clay, they shall mingle themselves with the seed of men; but they shall not cleave one to another, even as iron does not mingle with clay."

This is the explanation of these words given in A. R. 913:

By iron is signified the truths of faith, as was said; but when there is no truth of faith, but faith without truth, then the iron is mixed with miry clay, which do not cohere. By the seed of man, with which they should mingle themselves, the truth of the Word is signified. This is the state of the church at this day.

Swedenborg wrote these words, probably, in the year 1765.

Although, then, the Christian Church is represented particularly by the legs of iron, and its state of consummation when there is no faith remaining by the feet part of iron and part of clay, yet we are not to forget that the Christian Church has had its state of love or charity grounded in innocence represented by the head of gold, its state of faith represented by the breast and arms of silver, and its state of natural good represented by the belly and thighs of brass.

As to the preceding dispensations they must also have reached a state similar to the last state of the Christian Church, although it is with some difficulty that we apply the correspondence of the feet of iron mixed with miry clay to the lowest states of the Most Ancient Church and the Ancient Church respectively. Christians have been taught to think of the last state of the Jewish Church as the lowest of all, and the Lord's first advent as the period when a new humanity began to be formed. With many this idea still remains. They do not know that the first Christian Church has been spiritually consummated. The stone cut out of the mountain without hands, that smote the image and brake it in pieces, they believe to be Jesus Christ; but Swedenborg teaches that this stone or rock denotes the doctrine of the New Church revealed by the Lord at His Second Coming, by which a final judgment was executed upon the states of all in the world of spirits at that time (1757), and also upon the first Christian Church as it then existed in the world. The coming of the Lord in the spirit and power of His Word, "in all His glory," is foretold in the seventh chapter of Daniel where the "Ancient of Days" is spoken of as appearing after the beasts have risen from the sea.

We can have very little knowledge of the successive states of the Most Ancient Church and of the Ancient Church as they were manifested outwardly in the world. We know, however, that they, like the two succeeding dispensations came to an end from the loss of charity, or love, as the ruling principle of heavenly life. They successively declined from the celestial love of good which is the love of good for its own sake, or the purest form of it, to the spiritual love of good, to which man is led by the truths of faith, and then to the natural love of good to which man is led by obedience; and finally to the love of what was not good, but which they called good because it ministered to selfish delight and pleasure. The fall was not occasioned by one act of disobedience, but by successive departures from the centre of life. In the last state they corrupted all good and profaned every truth that remained — the iron was mixed with miry clay. This was the lowest state of each of these two dispensations — the Most Ancient and the Ancient — although the human race had not sunk so low as it did at the end of the Jewish and the Christian Dispensations.

In the Old Testament we have a literal history of the Jewish Church, not however full and connected. We may trace somewhat, in the Bible stories, the successive changes and final consummation of that church. The same general causes operated to produce its decline and consummation as in the former churches. It was not, however, a real church, but only the representative of a true church, having no spiritual faith or heavenly charity within it. And yet so long as its members preserved the outward forms of Divine worship which were prescribed to them under the Mosaic law, the church itself was preserved from destruction, but as soon as its members fell into disobedience and the open indulgence of evil, the church began to decline and finally came to an end. The judgment upon it took place when the Lord came into the world. The great image seen by Nebuchadnezzar in his dream was as fully representative of this church as of the two former ones.

Now when we come to the Christian Church, it would seem as if the facts of its history would supply us with the means of ascertaining whether its successive states were not also represented by the great image. But this can only be seen by those who view these facts in the light of the revelations made to the New Church. No one in the Christian world could fully know or understand the causes of the decline of the Christian Church, or believe that it came to an end spiritually, and was judged, unless the Lord had revealed such knowledge from heaven. There were no "wise men," none in the East or in the West, in any part of the Christian world, in the Greek, Roman Catholic, or Reformed Churches, who could read or understand the meaning of the great image, *maximus homo*, or the church viewed collectively as one man in the sight of the Lord. This is evident from the conflicting and erroneous interpretations which have been put upon this book called Daniel, and the Apocalypse.

Referring again to the little work called the "Coronis," we find that the four successive changes of state in each one of the above-named churches are said to be: "first the appearance of the Lord Jehovih and redemption, and the morning or rise of the church; second, its instruction, and its day or progression; third, its declension, and its evening or vastation; fourth, its end, and its night or consummation." Now in reference to the sources of knowledge respecting the changes in the Christian Church we read in the "Brief Continuation of the Coronis" the following:

The periodical changes which succeeded in the fourth or Christian Church are described in the Word both of the Old and New Testaments; in particular, its rise or morning is described in the Evangelists, in the Acts, and in the writings of the Apostles: its progression towards mid-day, in the ecclesiastical history of the first three centuries; its declension or evening, in the history of the following ages; and its vastation, and final consummation, or night, in the Apocalypse.

Here, then, we have the sources of information — the Word, the Apostolic writings, and the history of the Christian Church. The Apostolic writings and ecclesiastical history must be interpreted in the light of the revelations made to the New Church in order to be understood as the fulfilment of prophecy. To understand how the great image seen by Nebuchadnezzar in his dream typifies all the successive states of the Christian Church, we must study all these sources of information. The book called Daniel and the Apocalypse refer more particularly to the judgment upon this church, its consummation, and the coming of the Lord to establish a New Church. The Reformation is often taken as the beginning of a new era in the Christian Church, but it was only the beginning of the end. The age represented by gold did not extend as far as the third century, perhaps not longer than the time when the beloved apostle, John, passed into the spiritual world, or about the end of the first century. The second or silver age lasted until near the close of the third century, from whence it began to decline. The succeeding ages can only be defined as they are represented by the brass and the iron, by a careful study of ecclesiastical history.

As to the interpretation of the dream or the explanation given by Daniel, it must be observed that the king becomes the representative of the image. Here there is just as much need of a spiritual interpretation as in the language describing the dream itself. It is somewhat like the explanation of the parable of the Sower, given by the Lord, and that parable itself. Both need to be spiritually unfolded.

Nebuchadnezzar primarily represents the kingdom of love, which is the government of heaven and should be of the church on earth. Daniel said to him, "Thou art that head of gold." As the King of Babylon he represented the dominion of the Divine Love. This is the head of the image. There is a good love of dominion. It is the love of ruling for the sake of serving, or for the sake of use. When this love is turned to the opposite and becomes the love of ruling from the love of self, then the church comes to an end. So Nebuchadnezzar's kingdom came to an end. The second kingdom is not referred to as of silver, but the third is spoken of as of brass, and the fourth, it is said, shall be as "strong as iron." The different kingdoms simply denote the prevalence or rule of certain principles in the human mind, thus the successive states of the church, just as in the image. The "kingdom which shall never be destroyed" is the final reign of the Lord in His Divine Humanity as King of Kings and Lord of Lords. The truth which is revealed by Him at His Second Coming, especially the doctrine that His humanity is Divine, is compared to a stone cut out of the mountain without hands, because this doctrine is not derived from the self-derived intelligence of man, but from the Lord alone.

We are not to understand that the Divine homage paid to Daniel by Nebuchadnezzar represents the pure worship of the Lord. The worship of those who are represented by Nebuchadnezzar is not from a free and rational principle — it is not the worship of the Father in spirit and in truth. It is a compulsory worship from fear and not from love. Those who are in the love of dominion are governed by no other motive. They are compelled to acknowledge the power of Divine Truth, but they desire to make use of the knowledge they possess for their own power and gain.

CHAPTER III.

Nebuchadnezzar the king made an image of gold, whose height was three-score cubits, and the breadth thereof six cubits: he set it up in the plain of Dura, in the province of 2 Babylon. Then Nebuchadnezzar the king sent to gather together the satraps, the deputies, and the governors, the judges, the treasurers, the counsellors, the sheriffs, and all the rulers of the provinces, to come to the dedication of the 3 image which Nebuchadnezzar the king had set up. Then the satraps, the deputies, and the governors, the judges, the treasurers, the counsellors, the sheriffs, and all the rulers of the provinces, were gathered together unto the dedication of the image that Nebuchadnezzar the king had set up; and they stood before the image that Nebuchadnezzar had set 4 up. Then the herald cried aloud, To you it is commanded, 5 O peoples, nations, and languages, that at what time ye hear the sound of the cornet, flute, harp, sackbut, psaltery, dulcimer, and all kinds of music, ye fall down and worship the golden image that Nebuchadnezzar the king hath set up: 6 and whoso falleth not down and worshippeth shall the same hour be cast into the midst of a burning fiery furnace. 7 Therefore at that time, when all the peoples heard the sound of the cornet, flute, harp, sackbut, psaltery, and all kinds of music, all the peoples, the nations, and the languages, fell down and worshipped the golden image that Nebuchadnez-8 zar the king had set up. Wherefore at that time certain Chaldeans came near, and brought accusation against the 9 Jews. They answered and said to Nebuchadnezzar the king, 10 O king, live for ever. Thou, O king, hast made a decree, that every man that shall hear the sound of the cornet, flute, harp, sackbut, psaltery, and dulcimer, and all kinds of music,

11 shall fall down and worship the golden image: and whoso falleth not down and worshippeth, shall be cast into the
12 midst of a burning fiery furnace. There are certain Jews whom thou hast appointed over the affairs of the province of Babylon, Shadrach, Meshach, and Abednego; these men, O king, have not regarded thee: they serve not thy gods,
13 nor worship the golden image which thou hast set up. Then Nebuchadnezzar in *his* rage and fury commanded to bring Shadrach, Meshach, and Abednego. Then they brought
14 these men before the king. Nebuchadnezzar answered and said unto them, Is it of purpose, O Shadrach, Meshach, and Abednego, that ye serve not my god, nor worship the golden
15 image which I have set up? Now if ye be ready that at what time ye hear the sound of the cornet, flute, harp, sackbut, psaltery, and dulcimer, and all kinds of music, ye fall down and worship the image which I have made, *well*: but if ye worship not, ye shall be cast the same hour into the midst of a burning fiery furnace; and who is that god that
16 shall deliver you out of my hands? Shadrach, Meshach, and Abednego, answered and said to the king, O Nebuchadnezzar, we have no need to answer thee in this matter.
17 If it be *so*, our God whom we serve is able to deliver us from the burning fiery furnace; and he will deliver us out
18 of thine hand, O king. But if not, be it known unto thee, O king, that we will not serve thy gods, nor worship the
19 golden image which thou hast set up. Then was Nebuchadnezzar full of fury, and the form of his visage was changed against Shadrach, Meshach, and Abednego: *therefore* he spake, and commanded that they should heat the furnace seven times more than it was wont to be heated.
20 And he commanded certain mighty men that were in his army to bind Shadrach, Meshach, and Abednego, *and* to
21 cast them into the burning fiery furnace. Then these men

were bound in their hosen, their tunics, and their mantles, and their *other* garments, and were cast into the midst of 22 the burning fiery furnace. Therefore because the king's commandment was urgent, and the furnace exceeding hot, the flame of the fire slew those men that took up Shadrach, 23 Meshach, and Abednego. And these three men, Shadrach, Meshach, and Abednego, fell down bound into the midst of 24 the burning fiery furnace. Then Nebuchadnezzar the king was astonied, and rose up in haste: he spake and said unto his counsellors, Did not we cast three men bound into the midst of the fire? They answered and said unto the king, 25 True, O king. He answered and said, Lo, I see four men loose, walking in the midst of the fire, and they have no hurt; and the aspect of the fourth is like a son of the gods. 26 Then Nebuchadnezzar came near to the mouth of the burning fiery furnace: he spake and said, Shadrach, Meshach, and Abednego, ye servants of the Most High God, come forth, and come hither. Then Shadrach, Meshach, and 27 Abednego, came forth out of the midst of the fire. And the satraps, the deputies, and the governors, and the king's counsellors, being gathered together, saw these men, that the fire had no power upon their bodies, nor was the hair of their head singed, neither were their hosen changed, nor 28 had the smell of fire passed on them. Nebuchadnezzar spake and said, Blessed be the God of Shadrach, Meshach, and Abednego, who hath sent his angel, and delivered his servants that trusted in him, and have changed the king's word, and have yielded their bodies, that they might not 29 serve nor worship any god, except their own God. Therefore I make a decree, that every people, nation, and language, which speak any thing amiss against the God of Shadrach, Meshach, and Abednego, shall be cut in pieces, and their houses shall be made a dunghill: because there is

30 no other god that is able to deliver after this sort. Then the king promoted Shadrach, Meshach, and Abednego, in the province of Babylon.

REFERENCES.

Verses.	Numbers.
1, 2	P. P.
1–7	A. E. 1029
1–7 and following	A. R. 717; T. C. R. 754
1 and following	A. C. 1326
1 to end	L. J. 54
3–7	P. P.
8–12	P. P.
13–21	P. P.
22–25	P. P.
25–28	Dict. P. 11
26–33	P. P.
Chapter cited	2 Adver. 1719

COMMENTARY.

THE IMAGE OF GOLD AND THE FIERY FURNACE.

In studying the text of this chapter of Daniel, in connection with the references given to it by Swedenborg in his explanations of the Word, it is well to note that he adds to it three verses of the following chapter, giving to this one thirty-three verses, and making the thirty-third verse answer to verse three of chapter four. Nebuchadnezzar is a representative of the infernal love of dominion which endeavors to reduce all things into submission to itself, to gain power over the souls of men, and even to invade heaven itself. It may be said that this infernal love has prevailed in all ages and among all classes of men, unless we except the state of mankind before the fall, which was one of innocence and trust in the Lord.

It is customary to regard Babylon as a type of the Roman Catholic Religion. In the explanations given by Swedenborg he shows how the Roman Catholic Church, through the papal power, has exercised this unholy love and brought its members into entire subjection. When they have refused obedience to its decrees, it has pronounced excommunication upon them, and the punishments of hell have been held out to them as their lot after death. (See A. E. 1029.) The conduct of the rulers of this church is foretold in this chapter in what is said of the conduct of the Chaldeans, who accused the Jews of not worshipping the golden image which Nebuchadnezzar set up. (Verses 8-12.)

The Chaldeans denote those who are in falsities. The rage of the king against Shadrach, Meshach, and Abednego — called in the Hebrew tongue, Hananiah, Mishael, and Azariah — who were accused, knew no bounds, and he ordered these three men to be cast into the furnace of fire. The imagery prefigures the hatred of the rulers of the Church of Rome against those who would not obey them.

But we must not narrow down our interpretations to one age of the Christian Church. We should endeavor to learn not only its particular meaning with reference to one church or dispensation, but its larger and more universal meaning. Babylon, under the Hebrew form, Babel, is spoken of in Genesis, where the building of the tower of Babel is described. There it refers to the prevalence of the love of dominion in the Ancient Church, denoted by Noah, which came to an end from that cause.

The same infernal love prevailed in the Jewish Church. This church or its members would have been utterly destroyed, naturally as well as spiritually, had it not been kept alive by outward conformity to the law. It was necessary to preserve some knowledge of Jehovah through the written Word which was committed to their keeping. Their worship was profaned before the captivity, and at the best it had never been anything more than the semblance or outward representation of the pure worship of the Lord. In all the permissions of the Divine Providence He regards the preservation of the truth in some form as the final end. Had all knowledge of God been lost with the Jewish people or nation, a New Church could not have been raised up at the time of the Lord's coming on the earth. The final consummation of the Jewish Church through the love of dominion and the consequent profanation of the Word, is foretold in the prophecy of Isaiah, chapter four, under the figure of Babylon, and the Divine judgment upon it in chapters twenty-one, forty-seven, and forty-eight.

Babylon is also spoken of when the future state of the Christian Church is foretold in the Book of Revelation, called "The Apocalypse," particularly in the seventeenth chapter of that book, under the figure of a woman sitting upon a scarlet-colored beast. In the explanations of the meaning of the Apocalypse given to the New Church, it is declared that the woman thus described represents and signifies the Roman Catholic Religion, which, although originally founded upon the Word, was afterwards wholly corrupted and finally judged.

We have, therefore, types of this love of dominion in all parts of the Word, as it has been manifested in all the different churches and branches thereof. In the universal, spiritual meaning its corrupting influence is portrayed with reference to every individual man who suffers himself to be governed by it.

The story contained in this third chapter of Daniel illustrates in a vivid manner how this evil love endeavors to bring all men under its dominion, and, failing that, to visit them with cruel punishment; and, on the other hand, how those who are subjected to danger and sufferings are preserved from destruction by the Lord.

The king Nebuchadnezzar made a golden image, sixty cubits high and six cubits broad, and set it up in the plain of Dura in the province of Babylon. The image was probably gilded and not of solid gold. The measurements given are probably Babylonian, and may be taken as one hundred feet and ten feet, respectively, English measure. This gilded image is not described as to its form or features. It was doubtless in the human form and may have been an image of the king himself.

We know that it represents the love of dominion from the love of self which filled the heart of the king. From this inferral love he desired to have all nations and people bow down to him. He made himself a god. Gold corresponds to the good of love, the celestial principle which leads men to worship the Lord, to acknowledge all good to be from Him who is the highest good, and to desire that this good may be received by all. But when this good becomes adulterated, mixed with the evil of man's selfish nature and turned into its opposite, the gold denotes what may appear to be good in external form, but which is internally evil. It is like gilded fruit which is rotten within. With the evil the good they seek is their own pleasure, and their delight is to persuade others to accede to their wishes or to compel them to yield obedience to their commands. The worship of the golden calf by the Israelites was the lowest manifestation of this love which seeks its gratification in sensual and corporeal pleasures. All who are under the influence of the love of dominion springing from the love of self, give themselves up to such pleasures. History affords us notable examples of the vice and luxury of kings who have exercised despotic power.

It is not said that Nebuchadnezzar, at first, commanded all the people in his kingdom to worship this image. He sent and gathered all the princes, governors, captains, judges, treasurers, councillors, sheriffs, and all the rulers of the provinces, and commanded them to come to the dedication of the image. But when these officers were gathered together and stood before the image, the herald cried aloud and proclaimed to all people, nations, and languages present, that when they heard the sound of different musical instruments they should fall down and worship this image of gold. Whatever is done by a subordinate or agent, by command of another, is done by the will of the principal. Kings and potentates exercise dominion through their subordinates. The Pope of Rome executes his decrees through his cardinals, archbishops, and bishops; and these decrees are just as binding upon the people under them as if he were to command them directly in his own person.

He excites the affections of these subordinates so that they desire to exercise dominion themselves. The sounds of musical instruments correspond to the influence of a variety of affections, by which men are led to take delight in certain good or evil things. In this case, the affections of the people were excited to lead them to worship the golden image. Thus, according to the spiritual idea, men come under the influence of the love of self.

The love of ruling over others is often manifested in a stronger degree by a subordinate ruler than by a principal. But in whatever degree it may exist it always looks to self-elevation and not to the good of others. Where the freedom of others is not regarded, in the exercise of authority, government is not from heaven. No one can be led to good, except in a state of freedom and in the exercise of rationality. It is not difficult, therefore, to see that the worship of the golden image denotes the submission of the human will and understanding to the influence of self-love, either in ourselves or in others. Those who come under its influence are always ready to accuse others of evil, especially when others are not willing to yield submission to their personal authority. They become filled with the fire of hatred towards those who do not pay them homage, and act towards them with cruelty. The history of the Christian Church is filled with examples of this kind.

We are not to understand that this evil arises from the exercise of authority in one particular form of government more than in another. Whenever the government is that of the human will arbitrarily exercised without any law, that is, uninfluenced by the truth and without regard to the good of all, it is infernal, not heavenly.

The three men of the Jews who refused to bow down to the golden image, represent all those in the church who acknowledge and worship the Lord, and are therefore unwilling to come under the dominion of self-love whether exercised by one man or by many. This love, however, may become dominant in the individual without its being exercised directly over others. The idolatry of self is more dangerous than the worship of others. We may submit to the will of others and love them with natural affection for something which appears good in them. But, if we worship ourselves, we desire that all should honor, love, and obey us.

These three men of the Jews had all along refused to be fed with the king's meat. They received knowledge from their God, were governed by His spirit, and therefore could not worship any other. The command of the king to cast them into the furnace of fire is indicative of the burning hatred of the evil love of ruling over others exercised towards those who will not come under their dominion. As before remarked, the pains and torments of hell-fire were promised to those who did not confess that they believed in the decrees of the pope. But the Lord protects those who put their trust in Him. Latimer and Cranmer endured the torment of the flames while proclaiming their faith. It is declared in the narrative that these three men were cast into the furnace of fire "bound, in their hosen, their tunics, and their mantles, and their other garments," and that while those who cast them in were burned with the flame of the fire, the Jews came out unhurt; indeed, that "the fire had no power upon their bodies, nor was an hair of their head singed, neither were their hosen changed, nor had the smell of fire passed on them." This has been regarded by many as one of the most wonderful miracles recorded in the Bible. It seems to show that under certain conditions fire will not burn or destroy. If this is true spiritually, if men or spirits can be protected by the Lord from the fire of hatred and passion which would destroy them, cannot the same power, without violating any law of order, overcome the influence of the natural elements? "When thou walkest through the fire, thou shalt not be burned; neither shall the flame kindle upon thee." (Isa. xliii. 2.)

The human body can be protected from the action of heat by moisture. Men handle molten metal in this way. It is a little remarkable that some such idea seems to have been in the mind of the one who wrote the "Song of the three Hebrew Children" in the Apocryphal additions to the Book of Daniel, where we are told that they were "surrounded by a moist, whistling wind." May we not rather say that they were surrounded by a natural atmosphere, corresponding to the spiritual atmosphere, which was produced by the presence of angels, by whom they were protected. The Divine power overruled the action of the elements, as was the case when the Lord walked upon the Sea of Galilee and quelled the storm. The spiritual meaning seems to require actuality in the things recorded, otherwise there would be no basis for this meaning and we might be led to doubt the truth of the whole narrative. Some in the New Church have believed that the whole transaction took place in the spiritual world, and they confirm this idea by the statement in the narrative that when the king looked into the furnace he saw four men, and that the "form of the fourth was like the Son of God." The inference is that the spiritual sight of the king was opened — that he saw the spiritual forms of the three men, and the fourth form was that of an angel who was filled with the Divine Spirit or Presence, and is therefore called the "Son of God," according to the common version.

This commingling of natural scenes with spiritual ones is difficult to understand, although there are similar things in other parts of the Word, as in the case of Abraham entertaining three angels at the door of his tent. The theophanies of Scripture are too frequent to admit of denial unless we reject the Word entirely. Let us not, however, regard the term "Son of God" as the same as that used in the New Testament. In fact the correct translation is "son of the gods" — as in the text of the Revised Version. The fourth form, I take it, was that of an angel, and such an appearance could not have been an object of natural sight. Let us be careful, however, how we treat the Word in the letter, or do away with the literal statements of natural fact or spiritual phenomena. The statement is plainly made that the three men came forth out of the midst of the fire, and those who cast them into the fire were burned themselves — a fulfilment of the spiritual law that the evil which men would do to others returns upon themselves.

The king, when he saw that these men walked forth unhurt, commanded that they should be promoted in the province of Babylon. This may not be taken as an evidence of change of heart on the part of the king. Evil-minded men do from compulsion what they will not do voluntarily.

In conclusion we submit the caution to adhere to the mode of interpretation given in the writings of the New Church. Where it is stated in the letter of the Word that things were seen in vision, or where angels are mentioned as appearing to men, we must interpret such statements in the light of what is taught in the New Church of the relation of the natural world to the spiritual world and of man's spiritual nature and connection with that world, and not relegate to the domain of speculation what is clearly revealed by the Lord in His Holy Word.

CHAPTER IV.

Nebuchadnezzar the king, unto all the peoples, nations, and languages, that dwell in all the earth; peace be multi-
2 plied unto you. It hath seemed good unto me to shew the signs and wonders that the Most High God hath wrought
3 toward me. How great are his signs! and how mighty are his wonders! his kingdom is an everlasting kingdom, and his dominion is from generation to generation.
4 I Nebuchadnezzar was at rest in mine house, and flour-
5 ishing in my palace. I saw a dream which made me afraid: and the thoughts upon my bed and the visions of my head
6 troubled me. Therefore made I a decree to bring in all the wise men of Babylon before me, that they might make known
7 unto me the interpretation of the dream. Then came in the magicians, the enchanters, the Chaldeans, and the soothsayers: and I told the dream before them; but they did
8 not make known unto me the interpretation thereof. But at the last Daniel came in before me, whose name was Belteshazzar, according to the name of my god, and in whom is the spirit of the holy gods: and I told the dream before
9 him, *saying*, O Belteshazzar, master of the magicians, because I know that the spirit of the holy gods is in thee, and no secret troubleth thee, tell me the visions of my
10 dream that I have seen, and the interpretation thereof. Thus were the visions of my head upon my bed: I saw, and behold a tree in the midst of the earth, and the height thereof
11 was great. The tree grew, and was strong, and the height thereof reached unto heaven, and the sight thereof to the
12 end of all the earth. The leaves thereof were fair, and the fruit thereof much, and in it was meat for all: the beasts of the field had shadow under it, and the fowls of the heaven dwelt in the branches thereof, and all flesh was fed

13 of it. I saw in the visions of my head upon my bed, and, behold, a watcher and an holy one came down from heaven.
14 He cried aloud, and said thus, Hew down the tree, and cut off his branches, shake off his leaves, and scatter his fruit: let the beasts get away from under it, and the fowls
15 from his branches. Nevertheless leave the stump of his roots in the earth, even with a band of iron and brass, in the tender grass of the field; and let it be wet with the dew of heaven, and let his portion be with the beasts in the
16 grass of the earth: let his heart be changed from man's, and let a beast's heart be given unto him; and let seven times
17 pass over him. The sentence is by the decree of the watchers, and the demand by the word of the holy ones: to the intent that the living may know that the Most High ruleth in the kingdom of men, and giveth it to whomsoever he will, and
18 setteth up over it the lowest of men. This dream I king Nebuchadnezzar have seen: and thou, O Belteshazzar, declare the interpretation, forasmuch as all the wise men of my kingdom are not able to make known unto me the interpretation; but thou art able, for the spirit of the holy gods is in thee.
19 Then Daniel, whose name was Belteshazzar, was astonied for a while, and his thoughts troubled him. The king answered and said, Belteshazzar, let not the dream, or the interpretation, trouble thee. Belteshazzar answered and said, My lord, the dream be to them that hate thee, and the in-
20 terpretation thereof to thine adversaries. The tree that thou sawest, which grew, and was strong, whose height reached unto the heaven, and the sight thereof to all the earth;
21 whose leaves were fair, and the fruit thereof much, and in it was meat for all; under which the beasts of the field dwelt, and upon whose branches the fowls of the heaven
22 had their habitation: it is thou, O king, that art grown and

become strong: for thy greatness is grown, and reacheth unto heaven, and thy dominion to the end of the earth. 23 And whereas the king saw a watcher and an holy one coming down from heaven, and saying, Hew down the tree, and destroy it; nevertheless leave the stump of the roots thereof in the earth, even with a band of iron and brass, in the tender grass of the field; and let it be wet with the dew of heaven, and let his portion be with the beasts of the field, 24 till seven times pass over him; this is the interpretation, O king, and it is the decree of the Most High, which is come 25 upon my lord the king: that thou shalt be driven from men, and thy dwelling shall be with the beasts of the field, and thou shalt be made to eat grass as oxen, and shalt be wet with the dew of heaven, and seven times shall pass over thee; till thou know that the Most High ruleth in the king- 26 dom of men, and giveth it to whomsoever he will. And whereas they commanded to leave the stump of the tree roots; thy kingdom shall be sure unto thee, after that thou 27 shalt have known that the heavens do rule. Wherefore, O king, let my counsel be acceptable unto thee, and break off thy sins by righteousness, and thine iniquities by shewing mercy to the poor; if there may be a lengthening of thy 28 tranquillity. All this came upon the king Nebuchadnezzar. 29 At the end of twelve months he was walking in the royal 30 palace of Babylon. The king spake and said, Is not this great Babylon, which I have built for the royal dwelling place, by the might of my power, and for the glory of my majesty? 31 While the word was in the king's mouth, there fell a voice from heaven, *saying*, O king Nebuchadnezzar, to thee it is spoken: 32 the kingdom is departed from thee. And thou shalt be driven from men, and thy dwelling shall be with the beasts of the field; thou shalt be made to eat grass as oxen, and seven times shall pass over thee; until thou know that the Most High

ruleth in the kingdom of men, and giveth it to whomsoever
33 he will. The same hour was the thing fulfilled upon Nebuchadnezzar: and he was driven from men, and did eat grass as oxen, and his body was wet with the dew of heaven, till his hair was grown like eagles' *feathers*, and his nails
34 like birds' *claws*. And at the end of the days I Nebuchadnezzar lifted up mine eyes unto heaven, and mine understanding returned unto me, and I blessed the Most High, and I praised and honored him that liveth for ever; for his dominion is an everlasting dominion, and his kingdom from
35 generation to generation: and all the inhabitants of the earth are reputed as nothing: and he doeth according to his will in the army of heaven, and among the inhabitants of the earth: and none can stay his hand, or say unto him,
36 What doest thou? At the same time mine understanding returned unto me; and for the glory of my kingdom, my majesty and brightness returned unto me; and my counsellors and my lords sought unto me; and I was established in my kingdom, and excellent greatness was added unto me.
37 Now I Nebuchadnezzar praise and extol and honor the King of heaven; for all his works are truth, and his ways judgment; and those that walk in pride he is able to abase.

REFERENCES.

Verses.	Numbers.
1–4 .	. P. P.
1 to end .	. A. R. 717
3, 4 .	. A. C. 3762
5	. D. Lord 48
5, 6 .	. P. P.
6	. A. C. 5223
7–9 .	. A. E. 109; P. P.

7-11	A. C. 9553
7-13	A. R. 567; A. E. 650; Coronis 3
7-14	A. E. 1029
7-12, 14, 15	A. E. 1100
7-11, 17, 18	A. R. 757
7, 9, 11, 18	A. C. 5149
7, 19	A. E. 1029
8, 17	A. C. 9489
9	A. C. 3384; A. E. 662
9, 11	A. R. 936
9, 18	A. C. 776
10	A. C. 9229; A. R. 158; A. E. 204
10, 11	P. P.
10-13, 17-31	Dict. P. 11
10, 20	D. Lord 40; A. R. 173; T. C. R. 93
12, 13, 14	P. P.
13, 22, 29	A. C. 395, 9228; A. E. 257
14, 21, 31	A. C. 8153
15, 16	P. P.
17-19	A. E. 1029
17-30	P. P.
25, 26	T. C. R. 644
27	A. E. 1029
27-29	A. E. 650
29	A. C. 274
29-31	A. E. 1029
30	A. C. 3301; A. R. 47
31	A. C. 29; A. R. 60, 474
31-34	P. P.
34	A. E. 1029
Chapter cited	A. C. 1326

COMMENTARY.

NEBUCHADNEZZAR'S SECOND DREAM.

THE opening verses of the fourth chapter of the Book of Daniel, one to three, have reference to the decree which Nebuchadnezzar made, after witnessing the miracle of the saving of Shadrach, Meshach, and Abednego in the fiery furnace. They are in these words:

Nebuchadnezzar the King, unto all the peoples, nations, and languages, that dwell in all the earth : Peace be multiplied unto you. It hath seemed good unto me to shew the signs and wonders that the Most High God hath wrought towards me. How great are His signs ! and how mighty are His wonders ! His kingdom is an everlasting kingdom, and His dominion from generation to generation.

These words seem properly to belong to the preceding chapter, forming a conclusion to the wonderful miracle, and they are so placed by Swedenborg, as already noticed.

The language seems like the expression of a humble servant of the Lord ; the sincere acknowledgment of the Lord's power. Nebuchadnezzar was, no doubt, much impressed by what he had witnessed. But he was operated upon by fear, and not by love to the Lord. Those who are in the love of dominion are often compelled to acknowledge the Lord's power, although they have not ceased to love themselves, and to desire to exercise dominion over others. The language of the Popes of Rome has been full of this lip confession, while in their hearts they have thought of the power of Rome, and desired the submission of others to their decrees. There have been, of course, notable exceptions. This feeling, however, is almost inseparable from the exercise of arbitrary power. What follows in this chapter shows this.

The second dream of Nebuchadnezzar is a revelation of the state of his own life, and, in the higher spiritual meaning, it shows the spiritual state of the church, at the last times, when it is wholly given up to the love of dominion originating in the love of self. Some doubt has been expressed whether in his madness — which was of the species called lycanthropy (from two Greek words, *lukos*, a wolf, and *anthropos*, a man) — he actually led the life of a beast, or only imagined himself to do the things which Daniel predicted. From the language used by Swedenborg, in A. E. 1029, it would seem that we ought to accept the statement as it is given in this chapter literally, that is, as an historical fact, especially in verse 33, where the words of Daniel are declared to have been fulfilled. But the spiritual meaning is of course more important. We are told in the passage from the Apocalypse Explained, above cited, that "by the state of Nebuchadnezzar is described the state of those after death who extol themselves as gods over all things of the church, namely, that they are driven out from man, that is, that they are no longer men as to understanding; that they become beasts, and eat grass as oxen, and that their hairs grow like the eagles', and their nails like birds' claws, whereby is signified that they are altogether sensual, that in place of intelligence they have infatuation, and in place of wisdom insanity; to eat grass, to have hair like eagles' and nails like birds' claws, signifies to become sensual."

We can readily understand that in a state of insanity where there is a loss of all rationality a person may become in outward appearance like a beast, and may even act like one, snatching and eating grass, although he could not live upon it as food.

Let us now consider briefly this second dream of the king. As in the first dream, it is recited in full, as the king told it to Daniel, and it is then repeated as Daniel gave the interpretation, with the particulars, some of which are repeated again when the fulfilment is given. The dream and the interpretation are one.

The great tree which was strong and reached unto heaven has a double representation — it represents in the first place, Nebuchadnezzar himself, and all who, like him, are filled with the love of dominion and become insane from its lust; and, at the same time, it represents the church at its consummation when this love prevails.

As in the former case, the king called in the magicians, the astrologers, the Chaldeans, and the soothsayers to interpret the dream. One would suppose that they having failed to interpret his former dream, the king would not seek them again. This only shows, however, that those who do not fully believe in the Lord, and love Him, will, even after they have known from Divine revelation that the truth must be derived from the Word, still resort to external signs and proofs to know the will of God.

The correspondence of the tree to the church must be found in man himself, for the church is only a man in a larger form. The leaves of the tree are the thoughts and perceptions of the mind, which are at first connected with some knowledge of God, and thus have a fair appearance. It is said "the fruit was much," according to the Revised Version, but Swedenborg translates it, "the flower thereof much," which seems to refer to the blossoms from which the fruit comes. There is a correspondence here to works, because the fruit of a tree corresponds to the good which is done by man. But there are different kinds of works — those which are done from knowledge before it becomes fully united with the love of doing good to others, are only fruit blossoms which may never grow into fruit.

The beasts of the field and the fowls of the air are the affections of the mind and the thoughts of man which look to self; for this tree although it grew towards heaven, does not really represent the spiritual church. It cannot be said that the first Christian Church was a spiritual church. It did not have a true idea of the Lord in His Divine Humanity as the source of all life and power; consequently it fell away and became a prey to the love of dominion. Had the tree been good, it would have afforded shelter for all the harmless and innocent beasts and birds, and it would not have been hewn down.

In the process of time, when this church was fully consummated, a judgment was executed upon it. This judgment was accompanied by a new revelation of Divine truth. The Lord revealed Himself anew in order that the state of the church might be known. This is denoted by the "watcher" and the "holy one" who came down from heaven. The judgment was that this tree should be hewn down and destroyed, but the stump of the roots should be left in the earth, even with a band of iron and brass, in the tender grass of the field, and it is added, "let it be wet with the dew of heaven, and let his portion be with the beasts of the field until seven times pass over him."

When Daniel comes to interpret these words he applies them directly to the king, who is warned what his fate will be; but as Nebuchadnezzar and his kingdom represent the church, either in a state of purity filled with the genuine love of the Lord, or consummated and filled with the unholy love of dominion, we may properly understand these words as referring to the church at the time of its consummation, and the judgment upon it. The effect of every judgment is to remove all the mere appearances of religion, especially all external forms which are not in correspondence with heavenly internals. The Roman Catholic Church has maintained its power in the world through these very externals. When these are removed there remains nothing but the stump with the roots. These roots denote the different motives of the will from which the tree or the man has derived his power and life. If there be any remains of good, these will be kept alive by the dews of heaven — by influx of truth from the Lord into the internal degree of human life.

At the end of every church or dispensation there are these remains of good in the will from which a new church may be formed. But there must be a full consummation which is meant by the words, "seven times shall pass over him."

The love of dominion is suffered to continue and to exalt itself until it produces spiritual insanity. During this state the church is kept together by bands of brass and iron. When the king was walking in his palace twelve months after Daniel, called Belteshazzar, had interpreted this dream, and was exulting in his power and grandeur, the voice came from heaven telling him that the kingdom had departed from him, and in the same hour the judgment was fulfilled — and the king became an outlaw and a wanderer, losing his reason and becoming like a beast.

When man is left to himself, unrestrained by law, and all his natural passions burn within him, he loses all rationality. This will continue until the evil has spent its power, and then if there be still some good left, the Lord raises him up and he again becomes rational, obedient, loving, and wise. The return of Nebuchadnezzar to power seems to be confirmed by what remains to us of the history of those times, and I cannot but regard the concluding words of the chapter, where he ascribes honor and glory and dominion to the Lord, or the Most High, to be the expression of true worship, unless indeed, by the Most High, he meant his own god, Bel-Merodach. I think the representation changes after his return to reason. These last words of praise and honor are not those of a proud ecclesiastic or ruler, who still cherishes the love of dominion. The Babylonians, even, may become changed. The love of dominion originating in the love of self may become the love of ruling for the sake of serving. Certain it is that this must be the case with every one in whom the kingdom of heaven is established.

In verse seventeen of this chapter, we read these words :

The sentence is by the decree of the watchers, and the demand by the word of the holy ones ; to the intent that the living may know that the Most High ruleth in the kingdom of men, and giveth it to whomsoever He will, and setteth up over it the lowest of men.

It is a common belief that the Lord makes use of all kinds of instruments to accomplish His ends, and even permits evil men to do good that His kingdom may ultimately prevail. What is meant by the "lowest of men," in this verse, does not clearly appear, unless it refers to those who are suffered to rule, after those of the Babylonish character are removed. We have seen kingdoms fall and men of low degree assume the places of power that have been filled by the learned and the great. In all the changes of government the end which the Lord has in view is the final reign of His own truth and love in the hearts of men.

In regard to the interpretation of this dream by Daniel, we have a remarkable statement from Daniel himself. When the king saw that the dream troubled Daniel, he said : "Belteshazzar, let not the dream, or the interpretation, trouble thee." Belteshazzar answered and said : "The dream be to them that hate thee, and the interpretation thereof to thine adversaries.

The Word of the Lord is interpreted in one way by the good, and in the opposite way by the evil. The king's enemies are those who would confirm him in the love of dominion, and these are the evil spirits who continually act upon man's evil affections and endeavor to confirm him in evil through false persuasions. But the truth always reacts against those who pervert and profane it, so that while the Word is a light and protection to the good, it is the means of destruction to its enemies. Daniel's interpretation of the dream must be understood in this way, and our own application of it, as exhibiting the dangerous and deadly character of this evil love, should be to that love in ourselves, which is our greatest enemy, and is diametrically opposed to the love which reigns in the highest heaven, the love of ruling for the sake only of promoting the good of the Lord's kingdom.

CHAPTER V.

Belshazzar the king made a great feast to a thousand of
2 his lords, and drank wine before the thousand. Belshazzar,
whiles he tasted the wine, commanded to bring the golden
and silver vessels which Nebuchadnezzar his father had taken
out of the temple which was in Jerusalem; that the king
and his lords, his wives and his concubines, might drink
3 therein. Then they brought the golden vessels that were
taken out of the temple of the house of God which was at
Jerusalem; and the king and his lords, his wives and his
4 concubines, drank in them. They drank wine, and praised
the gods of gold, and of silver, of brass, of iron, of wood,
5 and of stone. In the same hour came forth the fingers of
a man's hand, and wrote over against the candlestick upon
the plaister of the wall of the king's palace: and the king
6 saw the part of the hand that wrote. Then the king's countenance was changed in him, and his thoughts troubled him;
and the joints of his loins were loosed, and his knees smote
7 one against another. The king cried aloud to bring in the
enchanters, the Chaldeans, and the soothsayers. The king
spake and said to the wise men of Babylon, Whosoever shall
read this writing, and shew me the interpretation thereof,
shall be clothed with purple, and have a chain of gold about
8 his neck, and shall be the third ruler in the kingdom. Then
came in all the king's wise men: but they could not read
the writing, nor make known to the king the interpretation.
9 Then was king Belshazzar greatly troubled, and his countenance was changed in him, and his lords were perplexed.
10 *Now* the queen by reason of the words of the king and his
lords came into the banquet house: the queen spake and
said, O king, live for ever; let not thy thoughts trouble thee,
11 nor let thy countenance be changed: there is a man in thy

kingdom, in whom is the spirit of the holy gods; and in the days of thy father light and understanding and wisdom, like the wisdom of the gods, was found in him: and the king Nebuchadnezzar thy father, the king, *I say*, thy father, made him master of the magicians, enchanters, Chaldeans,
12 and soothsayers; forasmuch as an excellent spirit, and knowledge, and understanding, interpreting of dreams, and shewing of dark sentences, and dissolving of doubts, were found in the same Daniel, whom the king named Belteshazzar. Now let Daniel be called, and he will shew the interpretation.
13 Then was Daniel brought in before the king. The king spake and said unto Daniel, Art thou that Daniel, which art of the children of the captivity of Judah, whom the king my
14 father brought out of Judah? I have heard of thee, that the spirit of the gods is in thee, and that light and understand-
15 ing and excellent wisdom is found in thee. And now the wise men, the enchanters, have been brought in before me, that they should read this writing, and make known unto me the interpretation thereof: but they could not shew the
16 interpretation of the thing. But I have heard of thee, that thou canst give interpretations, and dissolve doubts: now if thou canst read the writing, and make known to me the interpretation thereof, thou shalt be clothed with purple, and have a chain of gold about thy neck, and shalt be the third
17 ruler in the kingdom. Then Daniel answered and said before the king, Let thy gifts be to thyself, and give thy rewards to another; nevertheless I will read the writing unto the
18 king, and make known to him the interpretation. O thou king, the Most High God gave Nebuchadnezzar thy father
19 the kingdom, and greatness, and glory, and majesty: and because of the greatness that he gave him, all the peoples, nations, and languages trembled and feared before him:

whom he would he slew, and whom he would he kept alive;
and whom he would he raised up, and whom he would he
20 put down. But when his heart was lifted up, and his spirit
was hardened that he dealt proudly, he was deposed from
21 his kingly throne, and they took his glory from him: and
he was driven from the sons of men; and his heart was
made like the beasts, and his dwelling was with the wild
asses; he was fed with grass like oxen, and his body was
wet with the dew of heaven: until he knew that the Most
High God ruleth in the kingdom of men, and that he set-
22 teth up over it whomsoever he will. And thou his son, O
Belshazzar, hast not humbled thine heart, though thou knew-
23 est all this; but hast lifted up thyself against the Lord of
heaven; and they have brought the vessels of his house before thee, and thou and thy lords, thy wives and thy concubines, have drunk wine in them; and thou hast praised the
gods of silver, and gold, of brass, iron, wood, and stone,
which see not, nor hear, nor know: and the God in whose
hand thy breath is, and whose are all thy ways, hast thou
24 not glorified: then was the part of the hand sent from be-
25 fore him, and this writing was inscribed. And this is the
writing that was inscribed, MENE, MENE, TEKEL, UPHARSIN.
26 This is the interpretation of the thing: MENE; God hath
27 numbered thy kingdom, and brought it to an end. TEKEL;
thou art weighed in the balances, and art found wanting.
28 PERES; thy kingdom is divided, and given to the Medes
29 and Persians. Then commanded Belshazzar, and they
clothed Daniel with purple, and put a chain of gold about
his neck, and made proclamation concerning him, that he
30 should be the third ruler in the kingdom. In that night
31 Belshazzar the Chaldean king was slain. And Darius the
Mede received the kingdom, being about threescore and
two years old.

REFERENCES.

Verses.	Numbers.
1–4	P. P.
1–5 and following	A. R. 459
1 and following	A. E. 587
1 to end	A. C. 1326; L. J. 54; A. R. 717; A. E. 1029; Dict. P. 12
1, 2, 25–28	A. R. 313
2	A. R. 913
2–4	H. & H. 365; A. E. 220
2–5	A. R. 316
2 and following	A. C. 3079; A. E. 242
2–4 and following	A. C. 10227
2–5, 21	A. E. 376
2–4, 23	A. C. 8932
2–4, 25, 28	A. C. 9093
2, 5, 25, 26	A. E. 453
2, 5, 27	A. R. 364
3–5	A. C. 1183
5, 6	P. P.
7–9	P. P.
10–24	P. P.
11	A. C. 5223
11, 12, 14	D. L. & W. 383
12, 14	A. C. 9818; T. C. R. 156; A. E. 183
23	A. E. 1029
25	A. C. 10217
25–28	A. C. 3104; A. E. 373; P. P.
25, 30	A. R. 316
29, 30	P. P.
30	A. C. 3079
Chapter cited	T. C. R. 754

COMMENTARY.

BELSHAZZAR'S FEAST.

WE have considered what is said of Nebuchadnezzar in the first four chapters of this book of Daniel. This king now passes out of sight at the end of the fourth chapter. It is a little remarkable that nothing is said of his death. His reason returned to him, and it is said that "he praised, extolled, and honored the King of heaven," but we are not told how he came to his end.

When it is said of Nebuchadnezzar, "thou art this head of gold" (chap. ii. ver. 28), he represents the highest principle — the love of good derived from the Lord — and the desire that this principle should rule among men. But this principle when perverted becomes the love of dominion from the love of self, which destroys the church. The successive states of vastation through which the church passes, are denoted by the things that are related of Nebuchadnezzar. His insanity is that which arises from the exercise of this evil love. But he passed away before the final judgment came. He is believed to have reigned forty-four years.

A deeper state of evil, a lower degree of profanation was successively reached, and this is represented by what is said of Belshazzar, Regent of Babylon, the grandson of Nebuchadnezzar. There were four successors of Nebuchadnezzar who occupied the throne for brief periods after his death. These were Evil Merodach, Neriglissar, Laborosarchod, and Nabonidus.

The last named, a usurper, married a daughter of Nebuchadnezzar. His eldest son was Belshazzar (*prince of God*), who seems to have shared the throne with his father, or at least governed in the city of Babylon at the time of the invasion of Babylonia by the Medes and Persians under Cyrus. When this invasion began, and the invading army neared the city, Nabonidus fled to Borsippa, an outlying suburb of Babylon, where he submitted to the conquerors, while Belshazzar remained in the city, apparently ignorant of his impending fate.

In the light of these statements the apparent discrepancies in this fifth chapter of the book of Daniel are removed. The identity of Belshazzar with the son of Nabonidus is now established by the inscriptions on the clay cylinders discovered in Babylon.

What then does he represent, and what is the significance of that great feast and the words of judgment seen written upon the wall of the banquet chamber of his palace?

Belshazzar seems to have been a more degraded character than Nebuchadnezzar. He was given up to licentiousness and excess. Like the man spoken of in the Gospel, he said to himself, "Soul, take thine ease, eat, drink, and be merry," not knowing that the Lord would say, "Thou fool, this night thy soul shall be required of thee." The tendency of the love of self which seeks power in the world is to degrade man more and more until he gives himself up to the indulgence of his corporeal and sensual appetites and passions. The greatest tyrants have become like beasts. So debasing is the infernal lust of dominion. And when those who have known the sacred value of the truth and the holiness of heavenly things use these things to minister to their own pleasure and to gratify their ambition, they are guilty of the sin of profanation, out of which they cannot be delivered. The lot of profaners in the other life is the worst of all.

Now let us turn to the narrative. " Belshazzar made a feast to a thousand of his lords, and drank wine before the thousand." This is the initial verse of the chapter. The fact that nothing is related in this book of the previous life of Belshazzar, or of his acts and doings, or of the others who ruled after Nebuchadnezzar, does not require explanation. We need only refer to the general statement, already given in previous notes, that the Word was written for the sake of its spiritual meaning; that it is not, strictly speaking, a connected historical relation, and that only such things are recorded as are needed to convey spiritual truths relating to the church and to man's spiritual history.

A feast denotes the appropriation of good and true principles of life from the Lord, who is the source of all life, and at the same time the communication of these good and true things to others from a state of mutual love. But in an opposite sense it denotes the appropriation of what is evil and false.

When man profanes what is true and adulterates what is good, he takes delight in their opposites, and brings them forth in every possible form of self indulgence, associating with those who are in similar evil and falsity. To drink wine does not always mean to appropriate what is false; for wine in a good sense denotes truth derived from the Word and seen in spiritual light, that is in its relation to the good of life, while in an opposite sense it denotes truth falsified and used to confirm what is evil. This latter is the wine of Babylon, or the wine of abomination, with which the nations have become drunken. Those who are in the love of ruling over others come into states of spiritual drunkenness. The mention of a thousand lords, to whom Belshazzar made his feast, denotes a full and complete state of profanation, when every truth is falsified and every good adulterated.

This is the end or spiritual consummation of the Church, when the Lord is wholly rejected and every religious principle is denied, even though it may be outwardly acknowledged. This state can only be known to the Lord, or to those to whom He has revealed it.

What now follows in the text shows in what manner this evil of profanation takes hold of holy things that relate to the church and its Divine worship, and uses them to promote its own selfish delights.

Belshazzar, whiles he tasted the wine, commanded to bring the golden and silver vessels which his father, Nebuchadnezzar, had taken out of the temple which was in Jerusalem; that the king, and his lords, his wives and his concubines might drink therein. Then they brought the golden vessels that were taken out of the temple of the house of God which was at Jerusalem; and the king, and his lords, his wives and his concubines drank in them. They drank wine, and praised the gods of gold, and of silver, of brass, of iron, of wood, and of stone. (Ver. 2.)

Here we have exhibited the spirit of profanation and idolatry. The vessels of gold and silver which had been used in the temple service at Jerusalem represented the good and true principles from which man acknowledges and worships the Lord, and by which he is kept in a state of charity and faith. These Babylonians used these vessels for the purpose of gratifying their corporeal appetites, thus profaning holy things. In the representative worship of the Jewish Church these vessels themselves were holy because they contained the wine which corresponded to the pure and holy truths of the Word derived from the Lord, which nourish and sustain man's spiritual life. But now they were used as symbols of the false worship of those who are in the love of self. The good is mixed with evil and the true with the false.

The holy vessels in Jerusalem were carried away more than once. Ahaz took the silver and the gold from the house of the Lord and sent it to the Kings of Assyria (2 KINGS xvi. 8), Nebuchadnezzar took away what remained (DAN. ii. 2. See also JER. xxvi. 18–22; liii. 17, 24: 2 KINGS xxiv. 13). We read of their restoration in EZRA i. 7–11.

The gods of gold, silver, brass, iron, wood, and stone were real images or idols, and they correspond to the false imaginations and conceits of every degree, celestial, spiritual, and natural, derived from evil affection and a perverted application of the truth. The different degrees of good and truth, thus turned into evil and falsity, which become objects of man's affection and delight, are the gold and silver, the brass and iron, the wood and stone. The lowest state of evil and thus the end of the church is reached when all the principles of religion, even down to the things which relate to a man's natural life in the world, are made subservient to his selfish delight and pleasure. Whether we apply this to the individual life or to the church as a whole, we may see that the teaching is the same. The Christian Church reached its lowest state when its priests and rulers profaned its holiest truths and mixed them with their selfish evil loves, their very outer lives furnishing scenes of drunkenness and crime.

The time of visitation and judgment is now at hand.

In the same hour came forth the fingers of a man's hand and wrote over against the candlestick, upon the plaister of the wall of the king's palace, and the king saw the part of the hand that wrote. (Ver. 5.)

This was a revelation manifested by an outward spiritual appearance. It was an actual manifestation of the Divine power, a visitation of God preparatory to the final judgment that awaited the wicked and degraded king and people who were revelling in their mad passion and lust.

All judgment is effected by a revelation of Divine Truth, and in the spiritual meaning this is signified by the handwriting on the wall.

It was seen over against the candlestick, which represents the false light of a consummated church. This spiritual appearance was seen by Belshazzar, and it produced fear and trembling. "Then the king's countenance was changed, and his thoughts troubled him; and the joints of his loins were loosed, and his knees smote one against another." The effect of the light upon the wicked is to produce fear and to interrupt the influx of life, thus destroying their power. When man is deprived of the power of exercising his evil loves, his physical nature gives way and he becomes weak, the joints are loosened.

As in the case of Nebuchadnezzar's dreams, the astrologers, the Chaldeans, and the soothsayers are called in to read the writing and to give the interpretation. If we understand Babylon to mean the church, and particularly the Roman Catholic Church when it was sunk under the evil of the love of dominion by which its worship became profane and it came to an end, we will interpret the conduct of Belshazzar to represent the acts of the rulers of that church, previous to the Last Judgment, before the Lord had revealed the Heavenly Doctrines of the New Jerusalem.

They could not understand the spiritual meaning of the Word, in which the church is condemned as to its evil dominion. It is the same with every individual. When man becomes immersed in evil, he fails to see or to understand the signs of the coming judgment upon his own life. The wise men of Babylon represent the scholars and divines in the church who are appealed to to explain the meaning of the Word. The revelation must come from the Lord, who is represented by Daniel, and by those who are enlightened by Him. No others can open the book.

Now it is said that when these wise men failed, the queen said to the king, after reciting what Daniel had done in the reign of Nebuchadnezzar, "Let Daniel be called and he will shew the interpretation." The queen here represents the remaining affection in the church, from which some are led to seek the truth from the Word and to understand its meaning. Unless there were some remains of good at the end of the church none could be saved.

Daniel was gifted by the Lord with knowledge and wisdom which enabled him to see the handwriting and tell its meaning. His spiritual sight was opened, so that he could see the handwriting, and at the same time explain the meaning of the inscription: "Mene, Mene, Tekel, Upharsin." "Mene: God hath numbered thy kingdom and brought it to an end. Tekel: Thou art weighed in the balances and art found wanting. Peres: Thy kingdom is divided and given to the Medes and Persians."

Now we must not mistake the character of Daniel's vision, or attribute to him the power of understanding the spiritual meaning of this sentence as applicable to the state of the church at the time of its judgment. As in the case of Nebuchadnezzar's dreams and their interpretation, Daniel's language seems to point only to the downfall of an earthly kingdom. It did so point. This was its lowest meaning. But this earthly kingdom was representative, and purely so, of the reign of the evil love of dominion in the human heart wherever it prevails. The natural power is only a type of the spiritual, and this whole account was written for the sake of revealing the state of the church at its end, and not to give us the history of Belshazzar, as an earthly king.

The words, "God hath numbered thy kingdom and brought it to an end," have reference to the quality of the church signified by Babylon, that it is destitute of any truth; there was no truth remaining in it, at its consummation. To number, in the language of the Word, signifies to judge of the quality or state of the church as to truth. The Lord alone can do this. He alone reveals the state of the church. The handwriting on the wall is the Lord's own judgment made known in the Word. The words, "Thou art weighed in the balances and art found wanting," refer to the state of the church as to the principle of good; "thou art found wanting" meaning that there is no good remaining with those who are of the church. There was a complete vastation of the church, although there were some nominally members of it who were not spiritually a part of it. This was the case at the end of the Jewish Church.

The third clause of the sentence is, "Thy kingdom is divided and given to the Medes and Persians." Here we may again fall into the supposition that this language refers merely to the transfer of the Babylonian Empire to the Medo-Persian power. This transfer did take place, but such an event has little meaning for us now unless we see what it represents. Judgment upon the state of the church when it comes to an end is always followed by division and dispersion, and when one religion loses its sway over the minds of men another takes its place, but the final consummation does not come until both the will and understanding are destroyed, when there is no longer remaining any love of good or any understanding of truth. The power of Babylon was overthrown in the night, and Belshazzar was slain. But the kingdom was transferred to another who was not less inclined to claim the homage of men. We are told in the sixth chapter that Darius, the Mede, required to be worshipped as a god. This was profanation, but it was that kind of profanation which comes from the exaltation of the human intellect.

Looking for a fulfilment of these sayings of the book of Daniel in the history of the Christian Church, we see that when the church came to an end through the exercise of the love of dominion with the Roman Catholics, then faith alone reared its head, and it was not until this kingdom of error was set up, which was also accompanied by the loss of charity, that the final consummation came, and the judgment was fulfilled, signified by the words of the handwriting on the wall of the king's palace. The kings of Media and Persia, we are told, represent those who are in faith separate from charity. (See *Doctrine concerning Faith*, No. 66.)

But the reign of Cyrus, who conquered so many kingdoms and restored the Jews to their own land, has another and a different meaning, as we shall show hereafter.

The command of Belshazzar to clothe Daniel with scarlet, to put a gold chain about his neck, and to make him the third ruler in the kingdom, is only the enforced respect of one who is compelled to acknowledge the power of Divine truth against the desires of his own heart. The particulars of the capture of the City of Babylon by the invading army by night, are not given in this book, although secular history tells us that the forces gained entrance into the city by turning the waters of the Euphrates into a lake. The magnificence and grandeur of this great city, the descriptions of which almost exceed belief, find some confirmation in the allusions to it in the Book of Revelation, where it symbolizes the power of the church in which the evil of dominion holds absolute sway.

This is Babylon the Great which has fallen. (See JER. ii., REV. xvii. and xviii.)

It is worthy of note that the thirty-first or concluding verse of the fifth chapter of this book of Daniel is placed by Swedenborg as the initial verse of the sixth chapter. And this seems to be its proper place, if the arrangement into chapters is to be regarded, for it tells of the beginning of the new reign.

"And Darius the Median took the kingdom, being about three score and two years old."

CHAPTER VI.

It pleased Darius to set over the kingdom an hundred and twenty satraps, which should be throughout the whole king-
2 dom; and over them three presidents, of whom Daniel was one; that these satraps might give account unto them, and
3 that the king should have no damage. Then this Daniel was distinguished above the presidents and the satraps, because an excellent spirit was in him; and the king thought to set
4 him over the whole realm. Then the presidents and the satraps sought to find occasion against Daniel as touching the kingdom; but they could find none occasion nor fault; forasmuch as he was faithful, neither was there any error or
5 fault found in him. Then said these men, We shall not find any occasion against this Daniel, except we find it against
6 him concerning the law of his God. Then these presidents and satraps assembled together to the king, and said thus
7 unto him, King Darius, live for ever. All the presidents of the kingdom, the deputies and the satraps, the counsellors and the governors, have consulted together to establish a royal statute, and to make a strong interdict, that whosoever shall ask a petition of any god or man for thirty days, save
8 of thee, O king, he shall be cast into the den of lions. Now, O king, establish the interdict, and sign the writing, that it be not changed, according to the law of the Medes and
9 Persians which altereth not. Wherefore king Darius signed
10 the writing and the interdict. And when Daniel knew that the writing was signed, he went into his house; (now his windows were open in his chamber toward Jerusalem;) and he kneeled upon his knees three times a day, and prayed,
11 and gave thanks before his God, as he did aforetime. Then these men assembled together, and found Daniel making
12 petition and supplication before his God. Then they came

near, and spake before the king concerning the king's interdict; Hast thou not signed an interdict, that every man that shall make petition unto any god or man within thirty days, save unto thee, O king, shall be cast into the den of lions? The king answered and said, The thing is true, according to
13 the law of the Medes and Persians, which altereth not. Then answered they and said before the king, That Daniel, which is of the children of the captivity of Judah, regardeth not thee, O king, nor the interdict that thou hast signed, but
14 maketh his petition three times a day. Then the king, when he heard these words, was sore displeased, and set his heart on Daniel to deliver him : and he labored till the going
15 down of the sun to rescue him. Then these men assembled together unto the king, and said unto the king, Know, O king, that it is a law of the Medes and Persians, that no interdict nor statute which the king establisheth may be
16 changed. Then the king commanded, and they brought Daniel, and cast him into the den of lions. *Now* the king spake and said unto Daniel, Thy God whom thou servest
17 continually, he will deliver thee. And a stone was brought, and laid upon the mouth of the den ; and the king sealed it with his own signet, and with the signet of his lords ; that
18 nothing might be changed concerning Daniel. Then the king went to his palace, and passed the night fasting : neither were instruments of music brought before him : and his
19 sleep fled from him. Then the king arose very early in the
20 morning, and went in haste unto the den of lions. And when he came near unto the den to Daniel, he cried with a lamentable voice : the king spake and said to Daniel, O Daniel, servant of the living God, is thy God, whom thou
21 servest continually, able to deliver thee from the lions ? Then
22 said Daniel unto the king, O king, live for ever. My God hath sent his angel, and hath shut the lions' mouths, and they have not hurt me : forasmuch as before him innocency

was found in me; and also before thee, O king, have I done
23 no hurt. Then was the king exceeding glad, and commanded that they should take Daniel up out of the den. So Daniel was taken up out of the den, and no manner of hurt was found upon him, because he had trusted in his
24 God. And the king commanded, and they brought those men which had accused Daniel, and they cast them into the den of lions, them, their children, and their wives; and the lions had the mastery of them, and brake all their bones in pieces, or ever they came at the bottom of the den.
25 Then king Darius wrote unto all the peoples, nations, and languages, that dwell in all the earth; Peace be multiplied
26 unto you. I make a decree, that in all the dominion of my kingdom men tremble and fear before the God of Daniel: for he is the living God, and stedfast for ever, and his kingdom that which shall not be destroyed, and his dominion
27 shall be even unto the end: he delivereth and rescueth, and he worketh signs and wonders in heaven and in earth; who
28 hath delivered Daniel from the power of the lions. So this Daniel prospered in the reign of Darius, and in the reign of Cyrus the Persian.

REFERENCES.

Verses.	Numbers.
1–4	P. P.
1 to end	A. C. 1326
5–10	P. P.
8–10	A. E. 1029
8 to end	A. R. 717; T. C. R. 292, 754
11–18	P. P.
11, 14	A. C. 2788
19–24	P. P.
25	P. P.
26–29	P. P.
Chapter cited	A. C. 10412

COMMENTARY.

DANIEL IN THE LIONS' DEN.

In a former part of these commentaries, I have referred to the statement contained in the last verse of chapter v. (31) of the book of Daniel, which seems properly to belong to the beginning of the sixth chapter, as presenting some difficulty, when taken in connection with the history of Media and Babylonia. "And Darius, the Median, took the kingdom, being about three score and two years old." Now Cyrus was the conqueror of Babylon, and must have ruled over it in person or by a viceregent, as Babylonia had been ruled long before. I adopted the supposition that this Darius was some Median king or prince to whom the viceroyalty of Babylon was committed. The difficulty with several commentators has been to identify "Darius the Median," mentioned here, with any known character of history. The best supposition, it seems to me, is that supported by Mr. Westcott, that Darius was the personal name of Astyages, the last King of the Medes, who was the son of Cyaxares, the conqueror of Ninevah, the first Ahasuerus of Old-Testament history. In DANIEL ix. 1, Ahasuerus is said to be the father of Darius, the Mede. Cyrus was the grandson of Astyages by his daughter Mandane. According to the old legends, Astyages intended to put Cyrus to death secretly, but his life was preserved by the man who was expected to end it, and subsequently he was brought back to the king's palace, and was educated there, in Ecbatana, the capital city of Media. This was the youth who afterwards became the founder of the Persian Empire and a great warrior. Singularly enough, Astyages himself became subject to Cyrus, the latter having joined in a revolt of a party of the Medes against him and taken him prisoner. It is now understood by those who adopt the above supposition that Cyrus set his grandfather upon the throne of Babylon. This is not at all difficult of belief. Whoever this Darius the Median may have been, however, he did not rule long in Babylon. He must not be confounded with Darius Hystaspes, the Persian monarch of a later day, who sent great expeditions against the States of Asia Minor and Greece.

While it is not necessary to dwell at much length upon the history of those times in studying the spiritual meaning of this book, yet it seems useful to present a few facts to relieve the mind of apparent difficulties. We may be sure that "Darius the Median" was a real personage and that he represents some principle that rules in the mind when the church is consummated. The literal statements must not hold our attention too strongly if we would learn the spiritual ideas that are involved in them.

Let us turn to the narrative and consider the things that are recorded in this chapter. In the first three verses, as they are now placed in our Bibles, we read:

It pleased Darius to set over the kingdom one hundred and twenty princes which should be over the whole kingdom; and over these, three presidents, of whom Daniel was first, that the princes might give accounts unto them and the king should have no damage. Then this Daniel was preferred above the presidents and princes, because an excellent spirit was in him; and the king thought to set him over the whole realm.

In the Revised Version some slight changes have been made. The princes are called "satraps," a name applied to governors of provinces, who had great authority, but in all very important matters were wholly subject to the royal will and pleasure. Then they are said to be "throughout" the whole kingdom, and not "over" it. Again we read that Daniel was "one" of the presidents and not the "first." Now this arrangement or order of things under Darius, while it seems to relate only to civil affairs, represents the establishment of a government in spiritual affairs, or in the church, with a view to secure the obedience of human beings to the will of another, who is vested with absolute power, or to those under him, in order that he and they may receive adoration. It is the elevation of man to the throne of God. The worship of kings and emperors, which seems an incredible thing at this day, is not an unknown thing in history. Not a few have fancied themselves gods. Cæsar was proclaimed to be one, and when men refused to pay him Divine homage, the cry was heard, "To the lions." There seems, however, to be a difference between Darius and Cæsar. The former does not appear to have sought power or adoration. It was the presidents and satraps who sought occasion to accuse Daniel, although there was no fault in him, and to accomplish his destruction they prevailed upon Darius to sign the unalterable decree that no petition should be made to any god or man for thirty days, save to the king, and that whosoever did so should be cast into the den of lions. There is a striking analogy here to the conduct of the high-priests who sought occasion to accuse the Lord of seeking to overthrow the Roman government, and in Pilate we find a very striking resemblance to Darius. Indeed, in interpreting this portion of the book of Daniel, we should regard Darius as a representative of the civil power rather than of the spiritual, of the natural love of dominion as manifested in civil affairs, and the satraps and presidents as representing the priesthood who endeavor to gain power for themselves and who seek to obtain a decree or law which shall prevent the worship of the true God. Daniel, on the other hand, represents all those who acknowledge the Divine Truth and worship the Lord alone, and in the highest sense he represents the Lord who is the Divine Truth. The hatred and opposition of the high-priests and rulers in the Jewish Church to the Lord, and their desire to destroy Him, denotes the hatred of all who are in self-love and the evils which spring from it, towards the Divine Truth itself. The same natural feeling of pity which Pilate seems to have had for the Lord, making him unwilling to crucify him, seems to have influenced Darius. He placed Daniel in a high position, and "thought to set him over the whole realm." These rulers hated Daniel on this account. When they told the king of Daniel's praying to his God, "he was sore displeased and set his heart on Daniel to deliver him; and he labored until the going down of the sun to rescue him." But he could not reverse his own decree. When at last he allowed Daniel to be cast into the lions' den, he said unto Daniel, "Thy God whom thou servest continually, He will deliver thee," as if he believed in the power of God. To this may be added that he fasted all night and had no sleep after he had consented to the wicked deed. It is not an uncommon thing for men to act in this way. They are persuaded to do wrong against their better feelings and convictions, by designing men who flatter their pride and love of being exalted to power, and make them believe that human decrees are higher than the Divine Truth itself. The whole teaching of this chapter in its spiritual meaning points directly to the Roman Catholic Church, at the period of the Inquisition, when the Pope and his minions gained control over the civil power, and used it as a means to accomplish their own diabolical purposes.

Swedenborg plainly refers to the Inquisition as foretold in this chapter. "The punishment of the Inquisition," he says, "is the den of lions into which Daniel was cast." (See *Summary Exposition of the Internal Sense of the Prophecies and Psalms*.) The den of lions was not a natural den of wild beasts, but an artificial one in the king's forests where the beasts were kept to be hunted. It seems a horrible and cruel death to inflict upon human beings, to cast them to the lions to be devoured. This death was suffered by the Christians at Rome. Even more horrible were the punishments of the Inquisition in the fifteenth and sixteenth centuries, which are matters of history well known and authenticated. Death by the slow torture of the rack and the burning fagots was even more to be dreaded than the destruction by beasts.

All this evil passion and hatred springs from the infernal love of ruling over others. What a poor satisfaction it seems to us, in this age, to exact from our fellowmen a confession of our belief or to compel them to worship as we do! What a change has taken place in the Christian world! Although there may be men, even at this day, who entertain intense hatred against those who differ from them in their religious faith and form of worship, yet the civil power can no longer be used to gratify this hatred. The Inquisition is no longer possible.

The fact that Daniel escaped unhurt may be regarded as miraculous, but it is not difficult to see that the spiritual sphere of a human being, strong in his own faith, and guarded and protected by angels, would be felt by the beasts, who would quail under its influence. Daniel said: "My God hath sent his angel, and hath shut the lions' mouths, and they have not hurt me; forasmuch as before Him innocency was found in me; and also, before thee, O king, I have done no hurt."

The sequel proves the law of spiritual life that the evil which men would do to others returns upon themselves. The king commanded Daniel's enemies to be cast into the den of lions, and not only them but their wives and children; "and the lions had the mastery of them, and break all their bones in pieces, or ever they came at the bottom of the den."

The conduct of Darius in issuing the final decree that all men in his kingdom should tremble and fear before the God of Daniel, bears some resemblance to that of the civil rulers in the time of the Reformation who no longer favored the Church of Rome. This command can hardly be regarded as the expression of true spiritual worship, which springs from love and not from fear or compulsion.

Passing from the historical spiritual sense to a still higher meaning, let us consider this history somewhat with reference to the Lord's life. I have already pointed out the representation which Daniel holds throughout the whole narrative, how like he was to Joseph, who was held captive in a strange land, and yet became the saviour of his people by the power which God gave him to interpret dreams and to show forth his wisdom. His enemies were compelled to acknowledge this power even against themselves. From all that is written about Daniel, it is not difficult to see that he represents the Lord, and that all the sufferings he endured are typical of the temptations endured by the Saviour for the sake of redeeming man from the evil power. When the Lord was in the wilderness, it is said He was with the beasts. These beasts were the evil spirits of hell that sought His destruction. In the fifty-seventh psalm we read: "My soul is among lions: and I lie even among them that are set on fire, even the sons of men whose teeth are spears and arrows and their tongue a sharp sword." (Ver. 4.) These words signify spiritual temptations. Man's soul is among lions when he is tempted by evil spirits to deny the Lord and to disobey His commandments. Lions are destructive beasts. They are strong and powerful. In the language of the Word they sometimes denote the destructive power of falsity derived from evil, and sometimes the saving and redeeming power of truth derived from love. The psalmist, speaking of his spiritual enemies, says: "They gaped upon me with their mouths as a ravening and a roaring lion." (xxii. 13.) But the Lord Himself is called the "Lion of the tribe of Judah," by which is signified the omnipotence of the Divine Truth proceeding from the Divine Love. The Lord made the truth powerful in Himself to overcome all evil. Before this work was accomplished, however, He was tempted by evil spirits; His "soul was among lions," and unless He had been sustained by the power of Infinite Divine Love, hell would have gained the victory. Like Daniel He prayed not to any human power, but to the Divine power within Him. In the garden of Gethsemane He fell on His face and prayed three times, saying the same words: "O my Father, if this cup may not pass from me except I drink it, Thy will be done." (MATT. xxvi. 39-44.) Daniel seems to have had the words of the fifty-fifth psalm in his mind when he prayed three times a day from his windows with his face towards Jerusalem: "Evening, and morning, and at noon, will I pray, and cry aloud; and He shall hear my voice." (Ver. 17.)

When we speak of the lions' den as denoting hell, and the beasts as denoting the evil spirits of hell, we must think of a state of mind when man is assailed by those who would destroy his trust in the power of the Lord. The Lord's perfect innocence is simply represented by the innocence of Daniel, which must have been imperfect compared with the Divine Innocence itself. In the law of representation the spiritual quality of the one who represents is not to be reflected upon. We see the Divine only in faint images in the lives of those who exhibit heavenly virtue and angelic goodness.

Let us now briefly consider this narrative in relation to man's regeneration. Daniel not only represents the Lord as Divine Truth, he also represents the truth as it is received by man, or the spiritual principle seen with reference to his spiritual life. Darius, on the other hand, as the king or ruler in Babylon, represents the truth seen with reference to natural life, and as it may be made conducive to our natural welfare. Natural truth should be held subordinate to spiritual and Divine Truth; if not, man perverts and profanes holy things and is subject to Babylon. When man's affections are turned to evil and he is under the influence of self-love, he wishes to make all things subservient to himself. He thus sets himself against the Lord and is filled with hatred and enmity towards his neighbor. The truth loses its influence over his mind and he falls a prey to the influence of evil spirits. His spiritual life is in danger of destruction, because for a time he loses his freedom and rationality. But if there be remains of good in him and a remaining faith in the Lord, he will become conscious of the evil within him and around him, and will pray to the Lord for deliverance. He will set his face towards Jerusalem and pray at evening, morning, and at noon. The effect of spiritual temptation is to induce a fear of punishment and the loss of life. But the Lord is very near to man in temptation and is ever ready to save him, and if he constantly turns to the Lord for help, He will send His angel and shut the lions' mouths.

"No manner of hurt was found upon Daniel because he believed in his God." There is power in faith derived from love and united with it. And it is wonderful what an effect this power and the example of a good life have upon those who are in natural states of thought and have not yet acknowledged any spiritual law. This is shown in the speech and actions of Darius. The world is moved out of its indifference and unbelief by the results of good living and successful resistance to evil. And the natural man, looking to his own security and protection, may be willing to have the whole world acknowledge and worship the God of Daniel, when he sees that faith in Him gives men such power to overcome danger and evil, when it makes them masters over themselves and guides and teachers to others.

CHAPTER VII.

In the first year of Belshazzar king of Babylon Daniel had a dream and visions of his head upon his bed : then he wrote
2 the dream and told the sum of the matters. Daniel spake and said, I saw in my vision by night, and, behold, the four
3 winds of the heaven brake forth upon the great sea. And four great beasts came up from the sea, diverse one from
4 another. The first was like a lion, and had eagle's wings : I beheld till the wings thereof were plucked, and it was lifted up from the earth, and made to stand upon two feet
5 as a man, and a man's heart was given to it. And behold another beast, a second, like to a bear, and it was raised up on one side, and three ribs were in his mouth between his teeth : and they said thus unto it, Arise, devour much flesh.
6 After this I beheld, and lo another, like a leopard, which had upon the back of it four wings of a fowl : the beast had
7 also four heads; and dominion was given to it. After this I saw in the night visions, and behold a fourth beast, terrible and powerful, and strong exceedingly ; and it had great iron teeth : it devoured and brake in pieces, and stamped the residue with his feet : and it was diverse from all the beasts
8 that were before it ; and it had ten horns. I considered the horns, and, behold, there came up among them another horn, a little one, before which three of the first horns were plucked up by the roots: and, behold, in this horn were eyes like the eyes of a man, and a mouth speaking great
9 things. I beheld till thrones were placed, and one that was ancient of days did sit : his raiment was white as snow, and the hair of his head like pure wool ; his throne was fiery
10 flames, *and* the wheels thereof burning fire. A fiery stream issued and came forth from before him : thousand thousands ministered unto him, and ten thousand times ten thousand

stood before him: the judgement was set, and the books
11 were opened. I beheld at that time because of the voice
of the great words which the horn spake; I beheld even till
the beast was slain, and his body destroyed, and he was
12 given to be burned with fire. And as for the rest of the
beasts, their dominion was taken away: yet their lives were
13 prolonged for a season and a time. I saw in the night visions, and, behold, there came with the clouds of heaven one
like unto a son of man, and he came even to the ancient of
14 days, and they brought him near before him. And there
was given him dominion, and glory, and a kingdom, that
all the peoples, nations, and languages should serve him:
his dominion is an everlasting dominion, which shall not
pass away, and his kingdom that which shall not be destroyed.

15 As for me Daniel, my spirit was grieved in the midst of
16 my body, and the visions of my head troubled me. I came
near unto one of them that stood by, and asked him the
truth concerning all this. So he told me, and made me
17 know the interpretation of the things. These great beasts,
which are four, are four kings, which shall arise out of the
18 earth. But the saints of the Most High shall receive the
kingdom, and possess the kingdom for ever, even for ever
19 and ever. Then I desired to know the truth concerning
the fourth beast, which was diverse from all of them, exceeding terrible, whose teeth were of iron, and his nails of
brass; which devoured, brake in pieces, and stamped the
20 residue with his feet; and concerning the ten horns that
were on his head, and the other *horn* which came up, and
before which three fell; even that horn that had eyes, and
a mouth that spake great things, whose look was more stout
21 than his fellows. I beheld, and the same horn made war
22 with the saints, and prevailed against them; until the an-

cient of days came, and judgement was given to the saints of the Most High ; and the time came that the saints pos-
23 sessed the kingdom. Thus he said, The fourth beast shall be a fourth kingdom upon earth, which shall be diverse from all the kingdoms, and shall devour the whole earth, and shall
24 tread it down, and break it in pieces. And as for the ten horns, out of this kingdom shall ten kings arise ; and another shall arise after them ; and he shall be diverse from
25 the former, and he shall put down three kings. And he shall speak words against the Most High, and shall wear out the saints of the Most High : and he shall think to change the times and the law ; and they shall be given into his
26 hand until a time and times and half a time. But the judgement shall sit, and they shall take away his dominion,
27 to consume and to destroy it unto the end. And the kingdom and the dominion, and the greatness of the kingdoms under the whole heaven, shall be given to the people of the saints of the Most High : his kingdom is an everlasting
28 kingdom, and all dominions shall serve and obey him. Here is the end of the matter. As for me Daniel, my thoughts much troubled me, and my countenance was changed in me : but I kept the matter in my heart.

REFERENCES.

Verses.	Numbers.
1 and following	D. P. 134
1	. C. L. 26
1–3	P. P.
1–14	. T. C. R. 754
1 and following . . . D. Lord 52; A. R. 36, 945; T. C. R. 157, 851
1–14 and following	. A. R 717
1 to end . . . . A. C. 1326; Dict. P. 12

1, 2, 7, 13 . . D. Lord 52; D. P. 134; A. R. 36, 945; T. C. R. 157
2, 3 . . . . A. E. 418
2–7 . . . . A. E. 650
2, 3, and following . . . . A. R. 343
2, 7 . . . . A. C. 6000
3 . . . . T. C. R. 788
3, 4 . . . . A. C. 3901
3–7 . . . . A. R. 567, 574; A. E. 1029
3–9, 13, 14 and following . . . . Coronis 3
3, 7, 8, 20, 21–24 . . . . A. R. 270
3, 7, 8, 20, 21, 23–25 . . . . A. E. 316
4 . . . . A. E. 1029, P. P.
5 . . . . . A. R. 573; C. L. 193; A. E. 722, 781; P. P.
5, 7 . . . . A. E. 556
6 . . . . A. R. 572; A. E. 780; P. P.
7 . . . . A. R. 101, 435; P. P.
7, 8, 11, 19–25 . . . . A. C. 2832
7, 19 . . . . A. R. 49
7, 20, 24 . . . . D. Life 61; A. E. 675
7, 23 . . . . T. C. R. 761
8 . . . . A. C. 10182
9 A. C. 3301, 8215, 8459, 9470; D. S. S. 49; A. R. 47, 166, 694; T. C. R. 223; A. E. 67, 195, 253, 988; Diary 2; App. 10
9, 10 A. C. 934, 5313, 6832; A. R. 229, 287; A. E. 199, 336, 504; P. P.
10 . . . . A. C. 8620; A. R. 256
11 . . . . A. R. 748; P. P.
11, 12, 21, 24 . . . . A. C. 10182
12 . . . . P. P.
13 A. C. 1990, 9807; D. Lord 26; A. R. 24; T. C. R. 776; A. E. 36, 63, 594
13, 14 A. C. 49, 1607, 6752; A. R. 291, 478, 839; C. L. 81; T. C. R. 113, 416, 625, 788, 851; A. E. 175; P. P.
13–18, 27 . . . . A. R. 913
13, 14, 22, 27 . . . . Dict. P. 12
13, 14, 27 . . . . . . D. Lord 6, 42; A. R. 664; A. E. 1029
14 A. C. 4691; D. Lord 10; D. S. S. 86; A. R. 483, 523, 749; T. C. R. 251, 262, 288, 791; A. E. 331, 455, 468, 685; Ath. Cd. 19
14, 18, 27 . . . . A. C. 10248
15 . . . . D. Lord 48

15, 16	P. P
17, 18	P. P.
17 to end	A. C. 2547
17, 24	A. R. 720
18, 22	A. R. 749
18, 22, 25	A. C. 8153
18, 22, 27	A. R. 586
18, 27	A. R. 284
19	A. E. 70
19–21	P. P.
21	A. R. 586
22	D. Lord 4; P. P.
23	A. C. 1066; A. E. 697
23, 24	P. P.
23–25	A. E. 1029
24	A. C. 10182; A. E. 1034
25	A. R. 476, 799; A. E. 610; P. P.
26, 27	P. P.
27	A. C. 7051; A. R. 749; A. E. 685
28	P. P.
Chapter cited	A. C. 10455; H. & H. 171; A. R. 748; T. C. R. 760; Diary 2; App. 5

COMMENTARY.

DANIEL'S VISION OF THE FOUR BEASTS AND THE ANCIENT OF DAYS.

In the first year of Belshazzar, King of Babylon, Daniel had a dream and visions of his head upon his bed: then he wrote the dream and told the sum of the matters. (Ver. 1.)

In this initial verse, we have the prelude to what follows — a general statement in regard to a new revelation to Daniel, by a dream and vision.

As to the chronology of this chapter, the time when Daniel had this dream and vision, it is plain that the events narrated antedate the events related in chapter five. Some years elapsed between the death of Nebuchadnezzar and the first year of Belshazzar's reign.

The chronology of this book is not, however, of much importance to us. We have already stated the doctrine that the Word of the Lord was written solely for the sake of the spiritual sense and not for the purpose of recording natural events in a series. The succession is constantly broken. This may be seen even in the Gospel narratives. But the spiritual sense forms a connected unbroken chain. The arrangement of the different books of the Bible into chapters and verses is a modern thing, and it is possible that portions of different books have been chronologically misplaced. But we are chiefly concerned to find out the spiritual meaning. In the book of Daniel, as we have seen, there are three principal subjects treated of, namely, the vastation or consummation of the church, the judgment upon it, and the Lord's coming to effect this judgment and to establish a New Church.

What has been recorded in the previous chapters depicts the spiritual state of the church when the love of dominion prevails and man usurps the power of God. This is Babylon the Great. The church is then consummated. The natural rules over the spiritual, and the holy things of heaven and the church are profaned. But man is not allowed to go beyond certain limits. Evil destroys itself as Babylon was destroyed by an excess of luxury and self-indulgence. By an influx of Divine light which comes like a mighty wind the power of evil is overthrown, the wicked are cast down, and the Lord is manifested as the "mighty God" the "Everlasting Father." This is the judgment.

It will be noticed that the dream of Daniel is a new thing. He had been an interpreter of dreams before, but now he has a dream himself. In his dream he has the wonderful vision of the "four beasts ascending out of the sea" and "the Ancient of days." Let us not mistake the nature of Daniel's dream, or suppose that it has not a Divine meaning. Swedenborg clearly explains the nature of dreams. He says:

As to what relates to dreams it is well known that the Lord revealed the secrets of heaven to the prophets, not only by visions but also by dreams, and that dreams were equally representative and significative as visions, and that they were commonly of one sort; and further that things to come were discovered by dreams to others as well as to the prophets; as in the case of Joseph's dreams, and of the dreams of those who were with him in prison, and also of Pharaoh, of Nebuchadnezzar, and others. It may hence appear, that dreams of that sort come by influx from heaven as well as visions, with this difference, that the dreams come when the corporeal part is asleep, but visions when it is not asleep. In what manner prophetical dreams and such as are recorded in the Word flow in, yea, descend from heaven, has been shown to me to the life; concerning which I am at liberty to relate the following particulars.

There are three sorts of dreams. The first sort come mediately through heaven from the Lord; such were the prophetical dreams recorded in the Word. The second sort come by angelic spirits, particularly by those who are in front above, to the right, where are paradisiacal scenes; it was thence that the men of the Most Ancient Church had their dreams which were instructive (n. 1122). The third sort come by the spirits who are near when man is asleep, which also are significative. But phantastic dreams have another origin. (A. C. 1975, 1976.)

He describes at some length the manner in which dreams are produced. It is not necessary to give all the particulars here. The reader is referred to the work entitled "Arcana Cœlestia," in the numbers following those just quoted, where full explanations are given. It is evident that the dream of Daniel was of the first sort and came to him while he was asleep. He was upon his bed. It must be understood that with him there was an opening of his spiritual sight. The things which he describes were representations seen in the spiritual world. They typify the state of the church at its end and the coming of the Lord to judgment. What he saw he recorded and it became a part of Divine revelation, which remains to us at this day.

Let us turn now to the dream and the description of the things which he saw.

Daniel spake and said, I saw in my vision by night, and behold the four winds of the heaven brake forth upon the great sea. (Ver. 2.)

Let us remember we are now considering the state of the church at its end, and that the church on earth is connected with the spiritual world and derives its quality from those who are associated with it in that world. What Daniel described in such wonderful imagery, actually appeared to him in the spiritual world and pictured forth the states of evil and falsity, from which the church on earth derived its quality when the love of dominion prevailed and all manner of false doctrines filled the human mind.

The four winds breaking forth upon the sea represents the influx of the Divine spirit. The blowing of the wind is mentioned in the Word as an outward representation of the inflowing of the spirit of truth. The Spirit of Divine truth flows down through all the heavens, even to those who are in hell, but it is received according to the different states of angels, spirits, and men, and when it reaches those who are in states of evil it is resisted and turned into what is evil and false.

Now the great sea or deep represents hell, or the state of those who are in evil. It also represents the merely natural man in whose memory much knowledge may be stored up, but whose mind is not receptive of heavenly influences. The mind of every man is a heaven or a hell in miniature. What can come out of such a state but what is evil!

Daniel declares:

And four great beasts came up out of the sea diverse one from another. (Ver. 3.)

These four beasts represent the states of affection of those who are in evil, and the evils themselves which characterize the church at its end. A similar vision is recorded by John in the Book of Revelation, who says that he saw two beasts rise up out of the sea, one like unto a leopard with the feet of a bear and the mouth of a lion, and the other who had two horns like a lamb and spake like a dragon. (Chap. xiii.)

It is well known that man is compared in the Scriptures to certain beasts, as to his character or quality which is always according to his affection. Harmless and useful beasts typify the good affections in man — hurtful and useless beasts the evil affections.

Now these four beasts rising out of the sea, as seen by Daniel, specially represent the spiritual states of the men of the church at its consummation or end, which is denoted by night.

The church passes through successive changes or mutations. The first state is an intellectual one, in which man has power to think and to reason about the truths of the church and to soar upward in thought. This state is represented by the lion who had eagle's wings. At the commencement of every church the truth is received intellectually. In this state, man is apt to reason about truths and to regard them as his own. He is delighted with his new acquisitions and soars to heights of reasoning and speculation. But afterwards this merely intellectual state is passed, and man no longer feels the disposition to reason from his proprium — the intellectual power is subdued in him. This is signified by the wings being plucked. A true rational state succeeds. This is grounded in obedience and a knowledge and love of heavenly truths. This is meant by the image of the lion being "lifted up from the earth and made to stand upon two feet as a man," and a man's heart being given to it.

But this state does not remain. There is a descent or decline to a lower state. This is represented by the second beast.

And behold, another beast, a second, like to a bear, and it raised up itself on one side and it had three ribs in the mouth of it, between the teeth of it; and they said thus unto it, Arise, devour much flesh. (Ver. 5.)

When the church loses its power of understanding the Word rationally, it sinks into mere naturalism and literalism. The most heretical doctrines may be confirmed from the letter of the Word. The church, which is represented by Babylon, has confirmed its power by passages of the Word literally interpreted, as that the keys were given to Peter and by him handed down to his successors.

The vision of the bear with three ribs in its mouth is a symbol of the church in which all the hard literal truths of the Word are used to teach submission to the power of the church. By such teaching all rationality and freedom is taken away from man, and he is spiritually devoured or swallowed up, and is no longer capable of understanding anything spiritual.

After this I beheld, and lo, another, like a leopard, which had upon the back of it four wings of a fowl; the beast had also four heads; and dominion was given to it. (Ver. 6.)

The third state of the church here represented is that in which the false doctrines invented by its leaders are made to appear as true. The leopard is a treacherous animal; it has a beautiful skin, variegated with light and dark spots, which typify the falsification of truth, by which the most erroneous doctrines are made to appear true. When truths are thus falsified and confirmed by reasonings they become fixed and rooted, so that they cannot be changed. The prophet says: "Can the Ethiopian change his skin, or the leopard his spots?" (JER. xiii. 23.)

It is said that "the beast had four heads and dominion was given to it." Those who are represented by leopards were those in the Christian Church, especially among the clergy, who by false reasonings made their erroneous doctrines appear true to the minds of the simple, especially the doctrine of salvation by faith alone, without the works of charity. This doctrine obtained power at the time of the Reformation, and the leaders of the church at that day gained dominion over men's minds through the influence of that doctrine.

They laid claim to science, reason, intelligence, and wisdom, represented by the four heads of the beast by which they exercised power in the church. The four wings represented the power of reasoning and confirming what they teach.

The fourth beast is thus described:

After this I saw in the night visions and, behold, a fourth beast, dreadful and terrible, and strong exceedingly; and it had great iron teeth; it devoured and broke in pieces, and stamped the residue with the feet of it; and it was diverse from all the beasts that were before it; and it had ten horns. (Ver. 7.)

By this beast, we are told, is described the last state of the church, when there was no longer any good or truth remaining in it. This beast resembles the beast with its seven heads and ten horns mentioned in the seventeenth chapter of the book of Revelation. The church comes to an end when there is no longer any charity and consequently no genuine faith in the Lord.

By a horn is signified the power of truth from good, and, in the opposite sense, the power of falsity from evil. Here the horn is a symbol of the power of falsity, and the ten horns denote every kind of falsity. By the little horn mentioned in the eighth verse, which came up among them, is signified "the full and entire perversion of the Word by applying the literal sense to confirm the love of dominion." (A. E. 316.)

In this little horn there were "eyes like the eyes of man, and a mouth speaking great things."

With what power and eloquence have the great leaders of the church among the clergy proclaimed the doctrine that the power of the Lord to forgive sins has been granted to them. This doctrine has assumed many forms. Not only in the Papal dominion has it been taught. Wherever men have been taught to believe that there is any power to save in merely human beings, the Lord has been blasphemed and the church has come to an end. Because this state prevailed at the end of the church the Lord came again to manifest His power and glory and to save men from this great evil.

The vision which Daniel had of the Ancient of days is descriptive of the Lord in His Second Coming. It is similar to the vision of John. (Rev. i. 14.) By the coming of the Lord in the spirit and power of His Word, a judgment was effected. This is meant by the thrones having been cast down. The Lord as Divine Truth occupied the seat of power, instead of those who claimed power for themselves. "His throne was like the fiery flame and His wheels as a burning fire." This signifies that the Divine Truth proceeds from the Divine Love, which is like a consuming fire. Thus in the appearance of the "Son of Man" we have the Divine Truth represented by the whiteness of His garments and of His hair, and the Divine Love represented by the red and fiery flame.

In the thirteenth verse we read :

I saw in the night visions, and behold one like unto a son of man came with the clouds of heaven and came to the Ancient of days and they brought him near before him.

The term "Son of Man" is peculiar to the Gospel, and it is more correct to read *a* "son of man," as Daniel could not have used this expression with direct reference to the Lord as *the one Divine Man*, for He was not known as such before His coming in the flesh, although a coming Man was looked for, and thought of. The term "Ancient of days" means the Lord from eternity, or Jehovah. It also means the Lord as Divine Good, as the Son of Man means the Lord as to Divine Truth. (A. E. 199.) It has been suggested by some writers in endeavoring to explain the words, "they brought him near before him," that there is a distinction to be made between the "Ancient of days" and the "Son of Man," and that the word "they" refers to the angelic powers by whom the Son of Man or Christ was brought into union with the Father. But the Lord was not only the "Son born" and the "Child given," but the "Father of eternity." God was in Him and the Divine in Him was in the beginning with God. "I came forth from the Father and am come into the world. Again, I leave the world and go unto the Father."

To this "Son of Man" there was given "dominion and glory, and a kingdom, that all people, nations, and languages should serve Him. His dominion is an everlasting dominion, which shall not pass away, and His Kingdom that which shall not be destroyed." The Lord said, "All power is given to Me in heaven and on earth." By this power He was enabled to overcome all the power of evil at His first and at His Second Coming.

Daniel says :

As for me, Daniel, my spirit was grieved in the midst of my body and the visions of my head troubled me. (Ver. 15.)

The word "body" is better translated "sheath." The body is only a sheath or covering of the spirit. While man remains in the natural world the bodily senses often obscure the understanding of spiritual things. Daniel was troubled because he could not understand the vision. The interpretation was given to him, however, by further representations.

This interpretation needs to be explained by the law of correspondence. The images are repeated, but four kings are spoken of. Here we may fall into the same error that we pointed out in our notes upon the second chapter. The error is in speaking of the four kingdoms as if they referred to the four great monarchies of the East. These four kings do not refer to earthly powers, but to the evil and false influences which prevailed at the end of the church, which the Lord overcame at His Second Coming. "These great beasts which are four, are four kings which shall arise out of the earth." The mind is brought into utter confusion of thought by the attempt to identify these four kings with any earthly rulers. They simply represent and signify certain false principles which obtain dominion over the human mind, and the horns signify the destructive power of those principles. All these were finally overcome by the Lord, the "Horn of salvation," raised up for us in the house of his servant David.

The fourth beast, "exceeding dreadful," is a representative of the doctrine of salvation by faith alone. This is what made war with the saints until the Ancient of days came. Then the "judgment was given" and "the time came that the saints possessed the kingdom," that is, when the power of this false doctrine is overcome, all who are in the good of life are brought to a true knowledge of the Lord. To these the kingdom will be given after they have passed through trial and tribulation. The "former things" will "pass away" and a New Church will be established in which the Lord alone will be worshipped.

And the kingdom and the dominion, and the greatness of the kingdoms under the whole heaven shall be given to the people of the saints of the Most High: His kingdom is an everlasting kingdom and all dominions shall serve and obey Him. (Ver. 27.)

In reading these wonderful visions, doubts may arise in our minds, and we may be troubled, but if, like Daniel, we keep the matter in our hearts, the Lord will give us light and peace.

CHAPTER VIII.

In the third year of the reign of king Belshazzar a vision appeared unto me, even unto me Daniel, after that which 2 appeared unto me at the first. And I saw in the vision; now it was so, that when I saw, I was in Shushan the palace, which is in the province of Elam; and I saw in the vision, 3 and I was by the river Ulai. Then I lifted up mine eyes, and saw, and, behold, there stood before the river a ram which had two horns: and the two horns were high; but one was higher than the other, and the higher came up last. 4 I saw the ram pushing westward, and northward, and southward; and no beasts could stand before him, neither was there any that could deliver out of his hand; but he did 5 according to his will, and magnified himself. And as I was considering, behold an he-goat came from the west over the face of the whole earth, and touched not the ground: and 6 the goat had a notable horn between his eyes. And he came to the ram that had the two horns, which I saw standing before the river, and ran upon him in the fury of his power. 7 And I saw him come close unto the ram, and he was moved with choler against him, and smote the ram, and brake his two horns; and there was no power in the ram to stand before him: but he cast him down to the ground, and trampled upon him; and there was none that could deliver the ram 8 out of his hand. And the he-goat magnified himself exceedingly: and when he was strong, the great horn was broken; and instead of it there came up four notable *horns* 9 toward the four winds of heaven. And out of one of them came forth a little horn, which waxed exceeding great, toward the south, and toward the east, and toward the glorious 10 *land*. And it waxed great, even to the host of heaven; and some of the host and of the stars it cast down to the ground,

11 and trampled upon them. Yea, it magnified itself, even to the prince of the host; and it took away from him the continual *burnt offering*, and the place of his sanctuary was cast 12 down. And the host was given over *to it* together with the continual *burnt offering* through transgression; and it cast down truth to the ground, and it did *its pleasure* and pros-13 pered. Then I heard a holy one speaking; and another holy one said unto that certain one which spake, How long shall be the vision *concerning* the continual *burnt offering*, and the transgression that maketh desolate, to give both the 14 sanctuary and the host to be trodden under foot? And he said unto me, Unto two thousand and three hundred evenings *and* mornings; then shall the sanctuary be cleansed.

15 And it came to pass, when I, even I Daniel, had seen the vision, that I sought to understand it; and, behold, there 16 stood before me as the appearance of a man. And I heard a man's voice between *the banks of* Ulai, which called, and 17 said, Gabriel, make this man to understand the vision. So he came near where I stood; and when he came, I was affrighted, and fell upon my face; but he said unto me, Understand, O son of man; for the vision belongeth to the 18 time of the end. Now as he was speaking with me, I fell into a deep sleep with my face toward the ground: but he 19 touched me, and set me upright. And he said, Behold, I will make thee know what shall be in the latter time of the indignation: for it belongeth to the appointed time of the 20 end. The ram which thou sawest that had the two horns, 21 they are the kings of Media and Persia. And the rough he-goat is the king of Greece: and the great horn that is be-22 tween his eyes is the first king. And as for that which was broken, in the place whereof four stood up, four kingdoms 23 shall stand up out of the nation, but not with his power. And in the latter time of their kingdom, when the transgressors are

come to the full, a king of fierce countenance, and under-
24 standing dark sentences, shall stand up. And his power
shall be mighty, but not by his own power; and he shall
destroy wonderfully, and shall prosper and do *his pleasure:*
and he shall destroy the mighty ones and the holy people.
25 And through his policy he shall cause craft to prosper in his
hand; and he shall magnify himself in his heart, and in
their security shall he destroy many: he shall also stand up
against the prince of princes; but he shall be broken with-
26 out hand. And the vision of the evenings and mornings
which hath been told is true: but shut thou up the vision;
27 for it belongeth to many days *to come.* And I Daniel
fainted, and was sick certain days; then I rose up, and did
the king's business: and I was astonished at the vision, but
none understood it.

— — — ‥ —

REFERENCES.

Verses.	Numbers.
1	C. L. 26
1–3	P. P.
1–14 and following	A. E. 817
1 and following D. Lord, 52; D. P. 134; A. R. 36, 945; T. C. R. 157, 851	
1 to end	A. C. 411, 2832; Dict. P. 12
2 . . . . D. Lord, 52; D. P. 134; A. R. 36, 945; T. C. R. 157	
2–14 . . . . . D. F. 65, 66, 67; B. E. 83; T. C. R. 537	
3–21	A. C. 10182
3, 4, and following	A. C. 2830
3–5, 7–12, 21	A. E. 316
3–5, 7–12, 21, 25	A. R. 270
4	P. P.
4, 5, 9	A. C. 3708
5	P. P.
5–12	A. R. 586
5–25	A. E. 600

5–11, 25	A. C. 10132
5, 9, 10, 12	A. C. 4769
6–10	P. P.
7, 10	A. E. 632
8	A. E. 418
8–10	A. C. 9642
8–11	A. R. 51
9	A. C. 9815
9, 10	A. C. 1458, 1808, 2495, 4697
9–11	A. C. 5922; A. E. 72
9–13	A. C. 3448
9–14	A. C. 7988
10	A. C. 9408; A. E. 535
10–12	A. R. 711
10–13	A. C. 10042
10–14	A. R. 447; A. E. 573
10, 12	A. R. 541; A. E. 720
11	A. C. 9485
11, 12	P. P.
12	A. R. 51
13	A. C. 2838, 9229; A. E. 700
13, 14	A. C. 7844, 10134, 10135; P. P.
13, 14, 26	A. C. 2405
14	A. C. 8211; C. L. J. 13; A. E. 612
14, 26	A. C. 22, 2333; A. R. 151; T. C. R. 764; A. E. 179; Coronis, 5
15–19	P. P.
17	A. C. 9807; D. Lord, 28; A. E. 63
17, 19, 26	D. Lord, 4; Dict. P. 12
20–25	P. P.
20 to end	A. C. 2547
21	A. R. 34; A. E. 50
21, 23	A. R. 720
23	A. E. 412
23, 25	A. R. 586
26	C. L. J. 13; P. P.
27	P. P.

Chapter cited A. C. 10042, 10455; H. & H. 171; D. F. 61, 63; A. E. 716, 734; Diary, 2; App. 5

COMMENTARY.

THE RAM AND THE HE-GOAT.

IN this chapter we are told of a vision which Daniel had. By the "vision" we understand the opening of his spiritual sight, and not a dream. It may have occurred to him in the daytime. In point of time it must have been two years later than the dream recorded in the previous chapter. We read:

In the third year of the reign of King Belshazzar a vision appeared unto me, even unto me, Daniel, after that which appeared unto me at the first. And I saw in the vision: now it was so, when I saw, that I was in Shusan in the palace, which is in the province of Elam; and I saw in the vision, and I was by the river of Ulai. (Ver. 1.)

Shusan is supposed to be the same as Susa, the "city of lilies." It was formerly the capital of the country called Elam, which was a province of Babylon under Belshazzar. The word translated "palace" is the Hebrew form of the Persian *barû*, which means a fortress, or fortified castle. Commentators have supposed that Daniel had this vision in Susa, whither he had gone on business of the king; but there seems little reason for this supposition. He may have been acquainted with that city and visited it on official business at different times, but in his own home in Babylon, the city of Susa, the fortress and the river could have been seen; that is, the images of them in his own memory could have been called forth, while the vision itself of the ram and the he-goat, which were representative forms, was seen in the spiritual world. It was like that of the beasts rising out of the sea. The object of this vision was to depict the state of the Church in the future, and not the destinies of the kingdoms of Medo-Persia and Grecia, as has been supposed. The fact that symbolic figures, such as winged beasts with one or two horns, are found on Persian gems and cylinders, furnishes no ground for giving an interpretation to this vision which makes it apply to earthly affairs. Its meaning is purely spiritual, as much so as the Apocalypse. As to the mention of these earthly kingdoms in the latter part of this chapter, and the comparison made between them and the ram and goat, we shall speak presently.

The wars or combats mentioned in the Word signify spiritual conflicts or combats between what is true and what is false, or between good and evil. Here, in this vision of the ram and the he-goat, we have a representation of the great conflict between true faith on the one hand and a false faith on the other. The former is represented by the ram, the latter by the he-goat.

The ram, the male of the sheep, corresponds, in this vision, to the principle of faith united with charity, springing from a state of innocence, and it represents the Church in this state; while the horns denote the power of truth derived from good. The Lord compared His faithful followers to sheep. "I know My sheep and am known of Mine." "My sheep hear My voice and follow Me."

Faith is the spiritual principle of the Church. It is formed by means of truths derived from the Word and a life in obedience to them. Any one who has observed the habits of sheep may see how beautifully they symbolize the trusting and confiding followers of the Lord. Obedience, docility, patience, and trusting confidence are their marked traits. The true followers of the Lord who really constitute His Church possess spiritual qualities to which these natural traits correspond. We are led to believe from the history of the Church that the early Christians were of this character. The faith of the Church was pure so long as men believed in the Lord, loved Him, and obeyed Him. They forsook all and followed Him. The spiritual principle of faith, then, and those who have this principle in them, are symbolized by the ram with two horns seen by Daniel in vision.

All power is in good which manifests itself in and by the truth; or it is in truth derived from good. (A. C. 10182.)

These are the two horns of the ram, one somewhat higher than the other.

It is written:

I saw the ram pushing westward, and northward, and southward, so that no beast might stand before him; neither were there any that could deliver out of his hand: but he did according to his will and magnified himself. (Ver. 4.)

There is no doubt that the power of a genuine faith in the Lord increased and overcame many evils, from the time of the Lord's coming until the end of the first three centuries of the Christian era. No other power could stand against it. It pushed its way in different directions. The Christian Church, while it retained a pure faith in the Lord, continued to grow and flourish, extending from Asia into parts of Europe and Africa. But it is well known that Christianity declined and lost its pure faith in the Lord.

The decline of the Church is always due to the loss of charity and the exaltation of faith above it. This is foreshadowed in what is said in the following verses:

And as I was considering, behold an he-goat came from the west over the face of the whole earth, and touched not the ground: and the goat had a notable horn between his eyes. And he came to the ram that had the two horns, which I saw standing before the river, and ran upon him in the fury of his power. (Ver. 5, 6.)

As sheep and lambs are the symbols of charity and innocence and the faith which is derived from charity, goats are the symbols of what is opposite to this true faith; that is, faith alone which is always connected with pride and self-conceit. The he-goat thus represents the Church in its fallen condition, when its members are in the belief that salvation depends upon faith separate from charity and good works.

In the twenty-fifth chapter of Matthew, the Lord describes under the form of a parable the nature of the judgment. The sheep are set on the right hand and the goats on the left. The former are called and chosen while the latter are cast out. The Lord says, by the prophet Ezekiel:

And as for you, O my flock, thus saith the Lord God, Behold I judge between cattle and cattle, between the rams and he-goats. (Chap. xxxiv.)

Now it is wonderful how this doctrine of salvation by

faith alone has prevailed in all parts of the Christian Church, and how those who have become confirmed in it have opposed all who have not accepted it. It has many forms and phases. Not merely has it presented itself in the form of the dogma of salvation by faith in the merits of Christ's sufferings, but wherever men have cherished the idea that knowledge without love or without the works of charity is of saving efficacy, it has become antagonistic to the idea of simple faith in the Lord and obedience to His precepts. The pride and haughtiness of those who claim to be the sole possessors of the power of God by virtue of their retaining a knowledge, however perverted, of the revealed Word of God, and who deny the existence of a church outside of their own establishment is one form of this falsity, symbolized by the he-goat. The spirit of this false faith is destructive of religion, and it manifests a determined hostility towards those who oppose it.

And I saw him come close unto the ram, and he was moved with choler against him and smote the ram, and brake his two horns; and there was no power in the ram to stand before him, but he cast him down to the ground, and trampled upon him: and there was none that could deliver the ram out of his hand. (Ver. 7.)

There is no power in man to overcome falsity when it becomes deep-rooted and powerful. The Reformers were unable to overcome the power of Rome, and the Roman Church was unable to remove the false doctrine of salvation by faith alone. This dogma was broken into pieces by the very zeal and fury of those who advocated it; and out of this monstrous error many others sprang up at the end of the Christian Church.

We read:

And the he-goat magnified himself exceedingly; and when he was strong the great horn was broken; and instead of it came up four notable horns, towards the four winds of heaven. And out of one of them came forth a little horn which waxed exceeding great, toward the south, and toward the east, and toward the glorious *land*. And it waxed great even to the host of heaven; and it cast down some of the host and of the stars to the ground, and trampled upon them. (Ver. 8-10.)

The four horns which came up in the place of the great horn, which was first seen between the eyes of the he-goat, symbolize the numerous errors which have grown out of this original doctrine, as first taught by the Reformers, and afterwards mixed with evils which were made allowable. The tendency of all false teaching is to propagate new errors which divide and subdivide the Church. In connection with these four horns another one, a "little horn," is spoken of as growing out of them.

This "little horn" specially denotes the doctrine that man is justified when he believes in the vicarious atonement and substituted sacrifice. (See A. E. 632.) This doctrine of justification makes light of obedience, and even declares that man cannot keep the Commandments. How much it has grown, and what an influence it has had in creating division in the Christian Church and alienating men from each other, history abundantly shows. Faith alone always divides, especially when its advocates claim to be righteous or holy above others.

Its constant tendency is to destroy the influence of the Word itself and the truths which teach men to love the Lord and the neighbor. These truths of the Word are meant by the stars which the he-goat cast down to the ground and trampled upon. (For further explanation of the ram and he-goat, see *Doctrine concerning Faith*, 65–67.)

The "daily sacrifice" was "taken away" when men ceased to bring their religion into daily life and to make every act holy by devoting themselves to the service of the Lord and the neighbor. This profanation continued until it came to the full and a judgment was executed. This fulness of state is represented by "two thousand and three hundred days," or "evenings and mornings." No period of natural time could exactly express the duration on earth of this evil state of things in the church.

In the spiritual sense of the Word numbers have no natural application, but are used purely with reference to their spiritual signification. In this instance these numbers signify a fulness of state, when evil and falsity were united, and the sanctuary of religion was defiled, and the abomination of desolation stood in the holy place. (See MATT. xxiv. 15.)

The morning signifies the Lord, His coming, and the rise of a New Church. The evening signifies the last time of the church, when it is fully vastated. These are the subjects treated of in the spiritual sense of verses thirteen and fourteen.

From the fifteenth verse a new state of things is indicated:

And it came to pass when I, even I, Daniel, had seen the vision, that I sought to understand it; and, behold, there stood before me as the appearance of a man.

Here we see a similarity to the appearance of the Son of Man to John. The Lord is a Divine Man, and in all His manifestations to men, as recorded in the Word, He has appeared in a human form.

And I heard a man's voice between the banks of Ulai, which called and said, Gabriel, make this man to understand the vision.

As the man first spoken of represents the Lord, Gabriel represents a heavenly society, and especially a heavenly society which is in the knowledge respecting the Lord's advent, and that He is the God of heaven and earth. (See *ante* pp. 19, 20.)

The judgment is represented by the cleansing of the sanctuary. Daniel, as he stands by the River Ulai, seeking to understand the vision, represents those who are capable of being taught and instructed by the Lord.

In reality the vision and its explanation are one; that is, they contain the same spiritual ideas. By the appearance of the "man" is meant the appearance of the Lord, to reveal the truths of heaven from the Word. The river is the stream of truth which is contained in the Word, and the man's voice is the Spirit of the Lord speaking from it and making known the state of the church.

Daniel was actually brought into communication with a heavenly society, and received something of its light or knowledge. The appearance of the angel of the

Lord threw him at first into a state of fear, and he fell upon his face. Man in his natural state of life is unable to endure the appearance of angels. This is shown in other places in the Word. So Daniel not only fell upon his face, but fell into a deep sleep, which represents the state of the natural man. At the time of the Lord's Second Coming and the revelation of the spiritual meaning of the Word, the whole Christian world was in a state of mere naturalism. It required a new manifestation to awaken the world from this slumber.

Daniel, as a prophet, represents those to whom the Lord reveals Himself at His Second Coming, who having received the light become the means of communicating it to others. The angel touched Daniel and he stood upright.

Then follows what seems to be an explanation of the vision of the ram and the he-goat ; but the explanation is clothed in figurative language equally with the vision. It is very plain that they require to be explained together, as the dream of Nebuchadnezzar and its interpretation. We are not to understand that the whole of this wonderful vision has a limited application to earthly kingdoms which have long since passed away. A king represents some true or false principle, and a kingdom the government of that principle in the human mind. "The ram," it is said, "which thou sawest that had the two horns, they are the Kings of Media and Persia. And the rough he-goat is the King of Greece." This double analogy is used for the sake of bringing the spiritual meaning into a lower natural form of representation. The representative forms of the ram and the he-goat were appearances in the spiritual world; but the kingdoms of Media and Persia and of Greece were earthly kingdoms in which the spiritual principles represented by the ram and the he-goat were somewhat exhibited. But it is not to these kingdoms that the higher prophetic meaning refers. This was revealed for our "instruction in righteousness," to make known the state of the church, and not the facts of secular history. It would be very difficult to show how the Medo-Persian and Grecian kingdoms fulfilled the words of this prophecy. In fact, it is impossible. And what shall we say of the four kingdoms that shall stand up out of the nations, and of that "king of fierce countenance and understanding dark sentences," which stands for the "little horn," which we have seen denotes the false doctrine of justification by faith alone, which is full of dark mysteries.

It is written in verse 26:

And the vision of the evenings and mornings which hath been told is true: but shut thou up the vision; for it belongeth to many days to come.

These words apply to the certainty of the fulfilment of the prophecy, and to the fact that its meaning would be concealed until the time of its fulfilment; that is, at the end of the church.

Lastly, it is said:

And I, Daniel, fainted, and was sick certain days; then I rose up, and did the king's business: and I was astonished at the vision, but none understood it [or, there was none to make it understood].

This fainting and sickness represents a state of the

Christian world when there was a fainting of the spirits of men and sickness of the soul on account of the evils and falsities existing in the world. The Lord Himself passed through such states when He was in the world, and many souls have fainted and become sick at heart when they have seen and felt the desolation of the sanctuary. Nothing but a life of active usefulness will restore men to spiritual health. At this day there are many in such states, and they do not understand the prophecies and promises of the Word. The Bible is to many a closed book. "None understood it." But after this evening state the morning will arise and the vision will be understood. The Lord reveals at His Second Coming the spiritual meaning of those things that are "spoken of by Daniel the prophet," both as to the consummation of the old dispensation and the rising or coming in of the new. We may be, like Daniel, astonished at the vision, but if we look to the Lord and seek light from Him, He will make known to us the heavenly mysteries.

And the glory of the Lord shall be revealed, and all flesh shall see it together: for the mouth of the Lord hath spoken it. (Is. xl. 5.)

CHAPTER IX.

In the first year of Darius the son of Ahasuerus, of the seed of the Medes, which was made king over the realm of 2 the Chaldeans ; in the first year of his reign I Daniel understood by the books the number of the years, whereof the word of the Lord came to Jeremiah the prophet, for the accomplishing of the desolations of Jerusalem, even seventy 3 years. And I set my face unto the Lord God, to seek by prayer and supplications, with fasting, and sackcloth, and 4 ashes. And I prayed unto the LORD my God, and made confession, and said, O Lord, the great and dreadful God, which keepeth covenant and mercy with them that love him 5 and keep his commandments; we have sinned, and have dealt perversely, and have done wickedly, and have rebelled, even turning aside from thy precepts and from thy judge-6 ments: neither have we hearkened unto thy servants the prophets, which spake in thy name to our kings, our princes, 7 and our fathers, and to all the people of the land. O Lord, righteousness belongeth unto thee, but unto us confusion of face, as at this day; to the men of Judah, and to the inhabitants of Jerusalem, and unto all Israel, that are near, and that are far off, through all the countries whither thou hast driven them, because of their trespass that they have tres-8 passed against thee. O Lord, to us belongeth confusion of face, to our kings, to our princes, and to our fathers, because 9 we have sinned against thee. To the Lord our God belong mercies and forgivenesses; for we have rebelled against 10 him; neither have we obeyed the voice of the LORD our God, to walk in his laws, which he set before us by his ser-11 vants the prophets. Yea, all Israel have transgressed thy law, even turning aside, that they should not obey thy voice: therefore hath the curse been poured out upon us, and the

oath that is written in the law of Moses the servant of God;
12 for we have sinned against him. And he hath confirmed his words, which he spake against us, and against our judges that judged us, by bringing upon us a great evil: for under the whole heaven hath not been done as hath been done
13 upon Jerusalem. As it is written in the law of Moses, all this evil is come upon us: yet have we not intreated the favour of the LORD our God, that we should turn from our
14 iniquities, and have discernment in thy truth. Therefore hath the LORD watched over the evil, and brought it upon us: for the Lord our God is righteous in all his works which
15 he doeth, and we have not obeyed his voice. And now, O Lord our God, that hast brought thy people forth out of the land of Egypt with a mighty hand, and hast gotten thee renown, as at this day; we have sinned, we have done wick-
16 edly. O Lord, according to all thy righteousness, let thine anger and thy fury, I pray thee, be turned away from thy city Jerusalem, thy holy mountain: because for our sins, and for the iniquities of our fathers, Jerusalem and thy people are become a reproach to all that are round about
17 us. Now, therefore, O our God, hearken unto the prayer of thy servant, and to his supplications, and cause thy face to shine upon thy sanctuary that is desolate, for the Lord's
18 sake. O my God, incline thine ear, and hear; open thine eyes, and behold our desolations, and the city which is called by thy name: for we do not present our supplications before
19 thee for our righteousnesses, but for thy great mercies. O Lord, hear; O Lord, forgive; O Lord, hearken and do; defer not; for thine own sake. O my God, because thy city and thy people are called by thy name.
20 And whiles I was speaking, and praying, and confessing my sin and the sin of my people Israel, and presenting my supplication before the LORD my God for the holy mountain

21 of my God; yea, whiles I was speaking in prayer, the man Gabriel, whom I had seen in the vision at the beginning, being caused to fly swiftly, touched me about the time of
22 the evening oblation. And he instructed me, and talked with me, and said, O Daniel, I am now come forth to make
23 thee skilful of understanding. At the beginning of thy supplications the commandment went forth, and I am come to tell thee; for thou art greatly beloved: therefore consider
24 the matter, and understand the vision. Seventy weeks are decreed upon thy people and upon thy holy city, to finish transgression, and to make an end of sins, and to make reconciliation for iniquity, and to bring in everlasting righteousness, and to seal up vision and prophecy, and to anoint
25 the most holy. Know therefore and discern, that from the going forth of the commandment to restore and to build Jerusalem unto the anointed one, the prince, shall be seven weeks: and threescore and two weeks, it shall be built again,
26 with street and moat, even in troublous times. And after the threescore and two weeks shall the anointed one be cut off, and shall have nothing: and the people of the prince that shall come shall destroy the city and the sanctuary; and his end shall be with a flood, and even unto the end shall be
27 war; desolations are determined. And he shall make a firm covenant with many for one week: and for the half of the week he shall cause the sacrifice and the oblation to cease; and upon the wing of abominations *shall come* one that maketh desolate; and even unto the consummation, and that determined, shall *wrath* be poured out upon the desolator.

REFERENCES.

Verses.	Numbers.
1–3	P. P.
2, 13, 14, 20	Dict. P. 12
2, 25–27	Dict. P. 12
3	A. R. 492; A. E. 637
3, 4, 7–9, 16–19	Dict. P. 12
4–19	P. P.
10	A. R. 3; A. E. 409
11, 13	A. C. 6752; A. R. 662; A. E. 937
16	A. E. 405
17	A. C. 5585, 9306
18	A. C. 3869
20	A. E. 405
20–23	P. P.
21	D. Lord 52; D. P. 134; A. R. 36, 945; T. C. R. 157
24	A. C. 1857, 2025, 9680, 9715, 9954, 10129; D. P. 134; A. R. 779; A. E. 204, 375, 624; P. P.
24, 25	A. C. 395, 728, 6508; D. Lord 6
24–27	D. P. 328; A. E. 684
24 to end	A. C. 411
24, 27	A. C. 4535, 10497, 10622
25	A. C. 2336, 6508, 9228, 9954; D. Lord 64; A. R. 501, 880; B. E. 100; T. C. R. 782; A. E. 375, 652; P. P.; Dict. P. 12
26	A. C. 622; A. E. 315; Coronis 34; P. P.; Dict. P. 13
26, 27	A. E. 83
27	A. C. 988, 1857, 2180, 5376, 10042; A. R. 658, 757; B. E. 100; T. C. R. 179, 181, 378, 755, 758, 761, 782; A. E. 397, 1045, 1100; P. P.; Dict. P. 13
Chapter cited	H. & H. 171; C. L. 26; T. C. R. 851; Ath. Cd. 41

COMMENTARY.

DANIEL'S PRAYER AND THE DIVINE ANSWER.

In the explanation given of chapter six, we considered the questions in regard to Darius, who he was and what place he had in the history of those times. He is mentioned again at the opening of this chapter and also at the beginning of chapter eleven. Nothing need be added here respecting him.

The closing of Daniel's vision recorded in chapter eight left him in a state of grief and sickness. He felt the desolation that had come upon the Jewish Church and nation, and that would come upon the whole church of the future, and no doubt reflected deeply upon the vision he had seen. As one of those who had been carried into captivity, he knew what trials and sufferings had come upon his people in consequence of their own violations of the Divine commandments. These outward trials and sufferings were not only known to him but to Jeremiah the prophet; and to the latter it was revealed how long the Babylonish captivity would continue. This ninth chapter of the book of Daniel begins with these words:

In the first year of Darius, the son of Ahasuerus, of the seed of the Medes, which was made king over the realm of the Chaldeans: in the first year of his reign, I, Daniel, understood by the books the number of the years whereof the Word of the Lord came to Jeremiah, the prophet, for the accomplishing of the desolations of Jerusalem, even seventy years. (Ver. 1, 2.)

The period of the duration of the captivity was made

known to Daniel, not by a vision or a special revelation, but by the prophecy already declared by Jeremiah, which is recorded in the twenty-fifth chapter of that prophecy, verse 11 :

And this whole land shall be a desolation, and an astonishment; and these nations shall serve the King of Babylon seventy years.

And in chapter twenty-nine, verse 10, of the same prophecy, we read :

For thus saith the Lord, That after seventy years be accomplished for Babylon I will visit you, and perform my good word toward you, in causing you to return to this place.

It would appear that the manuscript rolls on which Jeremiah had written these things were known to Daniel and had been read by him as he says :

I, Daniel, understood by the *books* the number of the years whereof the Word of the Lord came to Jeremiah the prophet.

This may be thought to be doubtful, unless we believe that these manuscript rolls, or some of them, were carried to Babylon from Jerusalem, and there seems to be good ground for believing this. We are told that Jeremiah commanded Seraiah to read all the words he had written, when Seraiah and the other captives should come to Babylon. (See JER. li. 59–64.) We have no reason to doubt, however, that the period of the captivity was made known to the writer of the book in some way, and also the fact that the Lord would afterwards through Zerubbabel restore Jerusalem and rebuild the Temple.

Seventy years denotes a full period of profane worship, the vastation of the church and its consummation, thus it applies to the consummation of both the Jewish Church and the Christian Church. We have noted frequently the difficulty of applying the times mentioned in the Word to natural times, or the duration of earthly things. The same may be said in reference to the numbers seven and seventy. The effort to explain this book of Daniel literally has given rise to great confusion and error. As for instance what is said in verse twenty-five:

Know therefore and discern, that from the going forth of the commandment to restore and build Jerusalem, unto the Anointed One, the Prince, shall be seven weeks: and threescore and two weeks, it shall be built again, with street and moat, even in troublous times. (Ver. 25.)

Now the words "three score and two weeks" cannot be correctly applied to the time intervening between the restoration or rebuilding of Jerusalem and its Temple under the decree of Cyrus, and the coming of Messiah, who was the Lord, on earth. If we suppose, as some commentators have done, that the word "weeks," in this passage, means weeks of years or four hundred and thirty-four years, we are still in difficulty.

It may be asked if we interpret the numbers in one passage with reference to natural time, as the seventy years of captivity in Babylon, why not in the other passages? Ought not the rule of interpretation to be uniform? The answer will now be given. The seventy years of captivity had an actual and literal fulfilment in the history of the Jewish Church and people. The captivity lasted that period, and the end of it was near at hand when Daniel referred to Jeremiah's prophecy. This period was also representative of the complete state of profane worship in which the Jewish Church had sunk. The numbers seven and seventy in a good sense denote what is holy, and in the opposite sense what is profane. But this prophecy of Daniel extended beyond the period of the captivity, not only to the coming of Messiah or the Lord at the end of the Jewish Church, when all the Jewish representatives ceased, but even to the Second Coming of the Lord and the consummation of the first Christian Church. Indeed in its universal spiritual meaning, it refers to the desolation that comes upon every member of the church when he is carried away into captivity by the love of dominion, which originates in the love of self. The Lord then judges his life as He judges the evil state of the whole church in every age.

In this broad and universal application of the Word of prophecy to the state of the church in general and particular, we may see that natural times have only a correspondential meaning, and are not to be considered in any other way when we are interpreting the Word of the Lord. Even the seventy years of captivity which comprised an actual historical period are of little moment to us, only as they represent a state of complete vastation.

This idea may be still more clearly seen in the book of Revelation, the Apocalyptic book, which treats in its spiritual sense of the end or consummation of the first Christian Church, the Second Coming of the Lord, and the establishment of the New Jerusalem. We read in it that the number of those who were sealed was 144,000; that the number of the beast was 666, "the number of a man"; that the two witnesses should prophesy 1,260 days, and that afterwards their dead bodies should lie three and a half days "in the street of the great city, which spiritually is called Sodom and Egypt." Without a spiritual signification for these numbers, they have no meaning for us — we cannot understand them. But let us return to Daniel.

We find a change now in the narrative. After realizing the desolation of his people and their sin, he sets his face towards the Lord in prayer as he had done before, with his face towards Jerusalem. (Chap. vi. 10.)

This prayer of Daniel is full of the spirit of humility and repentance. As he felt the sin of Judah and Jerusalem he made supplication to the Lord for forgiveness. He prayed not for himself but for his people, for the restoration of Israel. He stands not merely as the representative of his people in this attitude of prayer and supplication, but of every devout and penitent soul who sees the sin of his own life and seeks, by prayer to the Lord, for power to overcome. At the end of every church there are a few left who still retain some faith in the Lord, and in states of innocence turn to Him for salvation.

In a still higher sense, Daniel here represents the Lord who wept over Jerusalem and prayed to the Father for the redemption of His people.

This prayer of Daniel from beginning to end is a confession of sin, and may serve as a model for all prayer; for in its spiritual sense it contains a full acknowledgment of the cause of evil and sin, that is, disobedience to the Divine law, and supplication that the power of the Lord may remove the evil or overcome its influence. In the mere letter there is the appearance of a visitation of the Divine vengeance — a punishment inflicted by the Lord.

Yea, all Israel have transgressed Thy law, even turning aside, that they should not obey Thy voice: therefore hath the curse been poured out upon us, and the oath that is written in the law of Moses, the servant of God, for we have sinned against Him. (Ver. 11.)

And again:

Therefore hath the Lord watched over the evil and brought it upon us. (Ver. 14.)

It must have appeared to Daniel, as it did to all the Jews, that the Lord inflicted punishment and suffering upon them because of their transgression and their sin, but in reality evil punishes itself; the Lord casts no one into hell, and He is ever ready to forgive. Yet it must appear to the natural mind that the Lord inflicts the punishment. A confession of sin is necessary on man's part that the door may be opened for the Lord to enter in, so that man may feel that He is mercy itself.

There was no spiritual change in the Jewish people as a church. Its worship was restored, but it never became a true church. It was only held back, as it were, and prevented from sinking into deeper evil, until the Lord came to judge it. All this was for the Divine end of the future salvation of the human race. The Jewish Church was restored and preserved on the earth, so that the knowledge of a Divine Being might not be lost. This was done through the written Word, in the histories and prophecies of which He is constantly spoken of, and the promise is given that He will come to rebuild the temple of humanity.

Now, beginning with the twentieth verse of this chapter, to the end of it, the answer is given to Daniel's prayer. He says:

And whiles I was speaking, and praying, and confessing my sin and the sin of my people Israel, and presenting my supplication before the Lord my God for the holy mountain of my God; yea, whiles I was speaking in prayer, even the man Gabriel, whom I had seen in the vision at the beginning, being caused to fly swiftly, touched me about the time of the evening oblation. (Ver. 20, 21.)

The angel Gabriel, as we have before explained, stands for a heavenly society with which Daniel was in communication, and this heavenly society which Gabriel represented was in the love of making known the truth respecting the Lord's coming. Gabriel is said to "fly swiftly," to denote the lively affection and desire of the angels that man should know the Lord in His Divine Humanity. He appeared to Daniel about the time of the evening oblation and touched him, to denote the communication of heaven with man even at the last time of the church, when his mind is turned to the Lord in holy worship.

Daniel said:

And he instructed me and talked with me and said, O Daniel, I am now come forth to make thee skilful of understanding. (Ver. 22.)

What was revealed to Daniel contained in its deeper sense the wisdom of the Lord concerning His coming to save the human race. This wisdom was concealed under the letter of the words which were spoken to Daniel. He saw only their natural meaning, which related to the restoration of the city of Jerusalem and rebuilding of the temple on the " holy mountain," for which he prayed; but in the heavenly meaning, which was known to the heavenly society with which he was in communication, this promise given in answer to prayer refers to every state of the church of the future and of the individual man, in which the Lord comes to enlighten and to save. It contains the Lord's answer to every prayer — the coming of the Lord, after every period of darkness and desolation, to restore and renew and rebuild the temple of humanity. And Daniel, to whom the answer is given, represents those who are in the sincere desire or love of the truth for its own sake and for the sake of amendment of life. Spiritual enlightenment is given to those who thus "seek the Lord while He may be found." Further the angel said to Daniel, that is, communication was given by an internal way, and at the same time Daniel heard an audible voice, saying:

At the beginning of thy supplications the commandment went forth, and I am come to tell thee; for thou art greatly beloved; therefore consider the matter, and understand the vision. (Ver. 23.)

As soon as man puts himself in the mental attitude of prayer, that is, when he turns his thoughts and affections to the Lord, influx is determined into his mind and he begins to see the truth and to feel the influence of the Divine Love. By "the commandment went forth" is meant that the Word of Divine Truth began to be opened so that its influence could be received. This is the effect of prayer. The degree to which man is enlightened and elevated must depend upon his previous states of instruction and regeneration, but every one who, in a state of innocence, looks to the Lord, receives light and guidance from Him.

The remaining verses, from the twenty-fourth to the twenty-seventh, we have already partly explained. In their lowest natural sense they have reference to the return from the captivity, the rebuilding of the city and temple, and afterwards to the coming of the Messiah and the judgment upon the Jewish Church. But the Jewish Church came to an end when the Lord came into the world. Then followed the first Christian Church. This also came to an end and was judged, as appears from the twenty-fourth chapter of Matthew and the Apocalypse. The Lord suffered the Jewish Church to remain until His coming, lest those who were in simple good should be destroyed with those who were only in external or seeming good. So it was at the end of the first Christian Church. This continuance is meant in the Gospel by suffering the tares and the wheat to "grow together until the harvest." The evil must come to the full before the judgment is effected and a New Church is established. The establishment of a New Church is meant by the rebuilding of Jerusalem. The decline of every church is caused by the loss of charity which is followed by the loss of true faith in the Lord. By the flood in the twenty-sixth verse is meant the breaking up of the church by false persuasions. "The Anointed One shall be cut off," that is as the Lord was crucified by the Jews so will all love to Him and faith in Him be extinguished. In the twenty-seventh verse we read:

And He shall make a firm covenant with many for one week; and for the half of the week, He shall cause the sacrifice and the oblation to cease; and upon the wing of abominations shall come one that maketh desolate, and even unto the consummation, and that determined, shall *wrath* be poured out upon the desolate.

This is the conclusion of the Divine message given to Daniel by the angel. It is a prophecy of the end of the church when "iniquity shall abound and the love of many shall wax cold."

It is often supposed by Protestants that the period of the Reformation was the beginning of a new era in the Christian Church. So it was. But this era did not restore the primitive faith in the Lord Jesus Christ nor bring peace and harmony into the world. It prevented the further increase of the Papal Dominion and opened the Bible in some lands to the common people. The Word, however, was not understood, false doctrines were drawn from it, and the Dragon cast a flood of waters over the earth. This short period of comparative purity and agreement with the truth was ended in the middle of the eighteenth century. This is predicted in these words: "And He shall make a firm covenant with many for one week." This is foretold also in the Apocalypse where the Roman Catholic and Reformed Churches are treated of with respect to their faith and worship. "For the half of the week," or "in the midst of the week," we are told, here in Daniel, "He shall cause the sacrifice and oblation to cease;" that is, the genuine worship of the Lord as the God of heaven and earth from true faith in Him and genuine love to Him came to an end. Lastly, it is written, "and for the overspreading of abominations, He shall make it desolate, even until the consummation, and that determined, *wrath* shall be poured upon the desolate."

In the Revised Version the "overspreading of abominations" is translated the "wing of abomination." Swedenborg translates it according to Schmidius, "upon the bird of abominations." The idea is that by mere reasonings and intellectual flights the men of the Reformed Churches brought in the doctrine of salvation by faith alone. This is the bird of abomination which brought desolation upon the church.

"Even to the consummation" signifies the last state of the church, where there will no longer be any truth or good remaining. Then the Last Judgment was executed in the world of spirits and a way was opened for the Lord's Second Coming in the spirit and power of His Word, by which a new church will be established in which the Lord alone will be worshipped.

That the consummation of the church at the time of the Last Judgment is thus predicted by the prophet Daniel appears from the Lord's words in the Gospel of Matthew, chapter twenty-four:

When ye, therefore, shall see the abomination of desolation, spoken of by Daniel the prophet, stand in the holy place (whoso readeth, let him understand), then let them which be in Judea flee into the mountains: let him which is on the housetop not come down to take anything out of his house: neither let him which is in the field return back to take his clothes.

CHAPTER X.

In the third year of Cyrus king of Persia a thing was revealed unto Daniel, whose name was called Belteshazzar; and the thing was true, even a great warfare: and he under-
2 stood the thing, and had understanding of the vision. In
3 those days I Daniel was mourning three whole weeks. I ate no pleasant bread, neither came flesh nor wine in my mouth, neither did I anoint myself at all, till three whole
4 weeks were fulfilled. And in the four and twentieth day of the first month, as I was by the side of the great river, which
5 is Hiddekel, I lifted up mine eyes, and looked, and behold a man clothed in linen, whose loins were girded with
6 pure gold of Uphaz: his body also was like the beryl, and his face as the appearance of lightning, and his eyes as lamps of fire, and his arms and his feet like in color to burnished brass, and the voice of his words like the
7 voice of a multitude. And I Daniel alone saw the vision: for the men that were with me saw not the vision; but a great quaking fell upon them, and they fled to hide them-
8 selves. So I was left alone, and saw this great vision, and there remained no strength in me: for my comeliness was turned in me into corruption, and I retained no strength.
9 Yet heard I the voice of his words: and when I heard the voice of his words, then I was fallen into a deep sleep on
10 my face, with my face toward the ground. And, behold, a hand touched me, which set me upon my knees and upon
11 the palms of my hands. And he said unto me, O Daniel, thou man greatly beloved, understand the words that I speak unto thee, and stand upright; for unto thee am I now sent: and when he had spoken this word unto me, I stood trem-
12 bling. Then said he unto me, Fear not, Daniel; for from the first day that thou didst set thine heart to understand,

and to humble thyself before thy God, thy words were heard:
13 and I am come for thy words' sake. But the prince of the kingdom of Persia withstood me one and twenty days; but, lo, Michael, one of the chief princes, came to help me:
14 and I remained there with the kings of Persia. Now I am come to make thee understand what shall befall thy people
15 in the latter days: for the vision is yet for *many* days. And when he had spoken unto me according to these words, I
16 set my face toward the ground, and was dumb. And, behold, one like the similitude of the sons of men touched my lips: then I opened my mouth, and spake and said unto him that stood before me, O my lord, by reason of the vision my sorrows are turned upon me, and I retain no strength.
17 For how can the servant of this my lord talk with this my lord? for as for me, straightway there remained no strength
18 in me, neither was there breath left in me. Then there touched me again one like the appearance of a man, and
19 he strengthened me. And he said, O man greatly beloved, fear not: peace be unto thee, be strong, yea, be strong. And when he spake unto me, I was strengthened, and said,
20 Let my lord speak; for thou hast strengthened me. Then said he, Knowest thou wherefore I am come unto thee? and now will I return to fight with the Prince of Persia: and
21 when I go forth, lo, the prince of Greece shall come. But I will tell thee that which is inscribed in the writing of truth: and there is none that holdeth with me against these, but Michael your prince.

REFERENCES.

Verses.	Numbers.
1–6	P. P
1, 7, 8	D. Lord, 52; D. P. 134; A. R. 36, 945; T. C. R. 157
2, 3	A. C. 2788
2–4	A. R. 505; A. E. 532
3	A. C. 9954; A. E. 375
4 and following	A. E. 79
5	A. C. 7601, 9881; A. R. 671; A. E. 951
5, 6	A. C. 425, 2162, 3021, 6135, 8813, 9406, 9872; A. R. 49, 468, 775; A. E. 69, 504; Dict. P. 50
5–12	A. R. 56; A. E. 77
6	A. R. 830
7–21	P. P.
10–12	A. C. 5376
10, 16, 18	A. C. 10130
12, 19	A. E. 80
13, 21	A. C. 1664; A. R. 548
14	Dict. P. 13
14, 15	D. Lord, 4
20	A. R. 34; A. E. 50
Chapter cited	A. C. 1664; H. & H. 171

COMMENTARY.

THE VISION BY THE RIVER HIDDEKEL, — A MAN CLOTHED IN LINEN.

A NEW revelation is made to Daniel; the captivity is nearly ended, and it is revealed to Daniel, after he has passed through a period of mourning and fasting, "what should befall his people in the latter days."

The chapter opens with this statement:

In the third year of Cyrus, King of Persia, a thing was revealed unto Daniel, whose name was called Belteshazzar; and the thing was true, even a great warfare: and he understood the thing and had understanding of the vision.

Daniel is again called by the name that was given to him at first by the prince of the eunuchs (chap i.).

The vision now recorded is said to have been given in the third year of Cyrus, King of Persia. Cyrus was the deliverer of the Jewish people. He was a great conqueror, first overcoming the Kingdom of Media, and uniting it with that of Persia, and then subduing and bringing under his dominion several other nations of Eastern Asia, including Babylonia, and at the same time breaking up the old religious customs. Nearly all Asia was thus subdued. Afterwards his son Cambyses conquered Egypt, which then became tributary to Persia, so that the latter became the most powerful kingdom of the East. There is much obscurity about the origin and history of Cyrus, but no doubt of the main facts above stated. In his character of deliverer of the Jewish people from their captivity to Babylon, he represents the

Lord. The return from the captivity was not only permitted by him, but commanded by an edict. (See EZRA i. 1–4.) This was done as some have supposed in recognition of the services rendered to him by the Jews, and also that Palestine might serve to protect his territory on the West. The Jews hailed him as their deliverer when he entered Babylon.

The return of the Jews to Jerusalem was carried out by Zerubbabel and Joshua, the son of Josedech.

Cyrus is mentioned in ISA. xliv. 28 and xlv. 1–3 :

That saith to Cyrus, He is my shepherd and shall perform all my pleasure : even saying of Jerusalem, She shall be built, and to the temple, Thy foundation shall be laid.

Thus saith Jehovah to His anointed, to Cyrus, whose right hand I have holden, to subdue nations before him ; and I will loose the loins of kings ; to open the doors before him and the gates shall not be shut ; I will go before thee and make the rugged places plain : I will break in pieces the doors of brass, and cut in sunder the bars of iron : and I will give thee the treasures of darkness, and hidden riches of secret places, that thou mayest know that I am the Lord, which call thee by thy name, even the God of Israel.

In these passages Cyrus is called the " Shepherd " and the " Anointed,' names which clearly refer to the Lord. In this prophecy of Isaiah, as in Daniel, he represents the Lord in His Divine Human life as the Saviour of the world. (See A. E. 298.)

Daniel understood the vision not as to its prophetic character and spiritual import, but in relation to the return from captivity, already decreed, which was to him a great deliverance for which he had constantly hoped and prayed; and also with reference to the restoration of Jerusalem and the rebuilding of the temple. Just previous to the vision Daniel mourned and fasted. He says:

In those days I, Daniel, was mourning three whole weeks. I ate no pleasant bread, neither came flesh nor wine into my mouth, neither did I anoint myself at all, till three whole weeks were fulfilled. (Ver. 2, 3.)

This mourning and fasting was on account of the evil impending and the fear lest his people would be destroyed. In relation to the Church and the individual man, it represents a full state of humiliation and a fear of damnation which precedes the manifestation of the Lord. The Church mourns when the Lord seems to be absent, and she rejoices when the Lord comes again to reveal Himself anew as the Divine Saviour and Redeemer. The vision which is now described in the succeeding verses — fourth and sixth — represents the coming of the Lord to restore the Church and to reveal Himself anew, first as a Divine Man, the "Word made flesh," and then in the Word transfigured or glorified by the unfolding of its spiritual meaning.

Daniel said:

And in the four and twentieth day of the first month as I was by the side of the great river, which is Hiddekel (*Tigris*). I lifted up mine eyes, and looked, and, behold, a man clothed in linen, whose loins were girded with pure gold of Uphaz. His body, also, was like the beryl, and his face as the appearance of lightning, and his eyes as lamps of fire, and his arms and his feet like in color to burnished brass, and the voice of his words like the voice of a multitude. (Ver. 4–6.)

We are at once struck with the similarity of this vision to that of John, recorded in the Book of Revelation. This has no doubt been noticed by every attentive reader of the Holy Scriptures. It is commented upon by Swedenborg as follows :

That it was the Lord who was thus seen by Daniel, plainly appears from the Revelation, where He was manifested before John in a manner nearly similar, concerning which it is said : " And in the midst of the seven candlesticks, one like unto the Son of Man, clothed with a garment down to the foot, and girt about the paps with a golden girdle. His head and His hairs were white like wool, as white as snow ; and His eyes were as a flame of fire. And His feet like unto fine brass, as if they burned in a furnace." (Rev. i. 13–15.) And again : " These things saith the Son of God, who hath His eyes like unto a flame of fire, and His feet are like fine brass." (ii. 18.) From the similarity of the description of the Son of Man seen by John in the midst of the seven candlesticks, and of the man clothed in linen, likewise of the Ancient of days seen by Daniel, it is evident that it was the Lord whom they both saw. His face being seen as lightning and His eyes as a flame of fire, signify, the Divine love of the Lord ; for the face with man is a representative image of the affection of his love, and especially so are the eyes, for from them the love shines forth, whence they sparkle as it were from fire. (A. E. 504.)

Now as to the nature of this manifestation it must be understood that the Lord does not appear to men or angels in His own Divine glory, but in a form accommodated to their state. He appeared before His incarnation, generally, in the form of an angel whose own individuality was laid aside, while he was filled with the Divine Presence, so that the angel himself knew not, for the time being, that he was not the Lord. (See A. C. 1925; H. H. 121; and D. L. W. 97.) Although it is expressly said by Swedenborg that it was the Lord who appeared unto Daniel, it must be understood, we think, that the man clothed in linen was an angelic appearance, according to the general teaching in the writings of the New Church. In the common version we read, "His body was like the beryl," but literally it is "like Tarshish," which is the country from which the shining gem called the beryl, supposed to be the chrysolite of the ancients and the topaz of the moderns, was obtained. The appearance of the man clothed in fine linen must be taken to represent the Lord as the Word, in which he manifests His glory at His Second Coming. The linen, as the Lord's raiment, denotes the Divine Truth with which He is forever arrayed. The Lord is to be thought of objectively, but also as to His essence and quality, especially as to His Divine Love and Wisdom. These, as they are manifested to our human thought, are denoted by the wonderful appearances spoken of. The gold of Uphaz or Ophir with which His loins were girded, His body like the beryl, His face having the appearance of lightning, His eyes as lamps of fire, and His arms and feet like in color to polished brass — all these are significative of the good of the Divine Love, which is manifested in the Truth, revealing His glory.

In A. C. 6135, where the above explanation is substantially given, it is also said:

By Tarshish, as the rest of the body appeared, namely the middle of the body between the head and loins, is signified the good of charity and faith, for Tarshish is a sparkling precious stone.

The polished brass which shines brightly from the arms and feet is significative of the Divine Love manifested in good deeds — the works of charity; while the eyes which shone as lamps of fire denote the Divine intelligence filled with love. Daniel saw this great vision as he stood by the side of the great river, the River Hiddekel, or Tigris. This river denotes the stream of Divine Truth as it proceeds from the Word and is seen by man in rational light.

Daniel says that he alone saw the vision. Others did not see it because their spiritual sight was not opened. Who those were who were with him we do not know. It is probable that as Daniel was now advanced in age he did not go about without attendants. These men who were with him were affected, however, by this spiritual presence, so that they quaked and fled to hide themselves. Daniel himself was so affected by the "great vision" that there was left no strength in him. Then, when he heard the words spoken to him, he had fallen into a sleep with his face toward the ground. We have only to refer to the account of the Transfiguration to find a parallel to this scene. The effect of the near presence of an angel is to produce fear and trembling. Instances in the Old Testament are familiar. The spiritual idea is that when the Lord comes to reveal the light of Divine truth, the effect is to produce a state of fear on account of the evil in the world. With the good, however, this is only temporary, for the Lord imparts strength to those who love Him. While man is in a merely natural state, he is filled with fear at every manifestation which comes to him from the spiritual world, but as soon as the spiritual degree of his mind is opened he passes out of sleep, he awakes to righteousness, and is touched by the influence of the Divine Love.

The Christian world was in the stupor of naturalism when the truths of the New Dispensation were revealed. Swedenborg was struck with terror at first at the wonderful things that were revealed to him, but he was raised to a state of spiritual illumination in which he was kept under the Divine guidance. It is hardly correct to say that the Jewish prophet represents the Swedish seer, but there is an analogy here. Every servant of the Lord, who, like Daniel, has kept the Lord's testimonies, is raised from the sleep of naturalism and is strengthened by the touch of the Divine spirit, so that he can hear the Divine voice calling to His beloved to stand upon his feet. It was told Daniel by the Lord when He thus appeared to him that He had been with him from the first day that he had set his heart to understand and to chasten himself. The Lord is always present with every one who is in the effort to know His will and do it, but He does not reveal Himself fully to the man of the Church, or to the Church as a whole, until there has been a full period of vastation and humiliation. Without the effort to learn the truth, and without sincere humiliation of the heart before the Lord when evil is made known, there can be no spiritual elevation. Daniel had prayed many times to the Lord, he had desired light in the darkness, and now the Lord answered his words. As a prophet, Daniel represents at one time the Lord, as when he interpreted the dream of Nebuchadnezzar, but now he represents the man of the Church to whom the Divine Truth is revealed. All the prophets sustained this double representation, standing as representatives of the Lord when they taught and prophesied, and representing the state of the Church when they were in suffering and humiliation. Moses also in the Word has a similar duality of representation. And, indeed, the Lord Himself passed through two distinct states, one of humiliation on the human side of His life in which He "bore the sins of many," and one of Divine glory in which He revealed the will of the Father and was "mighty to save." In verse 13 we read:

But the prince of the kingdom of Persia withstood me one and twenty days: but lo, Michael, one of the chief princes, came to help me; and I remained there with the Kings of Persia.

This language is descriptive not of an earthly conflict but of a spiritual one. It relates to "war in heaven," that is, on the spiritual side and not on earth. The Kings of Persia simply represent and signify the forces of evil and falsity which make war against the truth. Michael represents an angelic society, which is in the acknowledgment of the Divine Humanity and from which strength is derived. When the Lord was tempted and suffered, angels came and strengthened Him. (LUKE xxii. 43.) This portion of the prophecy seems to point clearly to the Lord's Second Coming, and Daniel's attitude represents a state of profound humility, which will be the state of all who receive the revelations made to the New Church. He "set his face towards the ground and was dumb."

Then we are told: "And behold, one, like the similitude of the sons of men touched my lips." It is said in verse 10 that a "hand touched him," when he first saw the vision, and there remained no strength in him. By the touch of the hand is signified the communication of power. Here by the lips being touched is meant the communication of truth. Isaiah declares that his lips were touched with a live coal from the altar, which signifies that the prophet was gifted with a degree of inspiration by the communication of the Divine Love. Daniel's mouth was then opened and he spake and said unto Him that stood before him: "O my Lord, by reason of the vision my sorrows are turned upon me, and I retain no strength. (Ver. 16.)

The effect of the opening of the spiritual degree of the mind to the light of Divine Truth, is to render man's lower nature weak and to bring him into the acknowledgment that of himself he is altogether nothing. This confession which Daniel made is that of every humble believer in the Lord, when the truth is clearly manifested. And then new strength is imparted by a new communication from above. (Ver. 18.) The form of the address to Daniel: "O man, greatly beloved, fear not: peace be unto thee, be strong, yea be strong" (ver. 19), shows how those who are faithful to the Lord's teachings are conjoined to Him by love and made strong in their faith. In every new revelation and in every consequent elevation of the understanding to receive it, there is necessarily a resistance from opposing forces. The spiritual combats against evil and falsity in which man must engage, do not cease with the reception of the highest truths, truths of a celestial kind; these truths cannot be ours, in fact, until the opposite falsities are removed, especially the great falsity which would lead us to believe that we have knowledge or power from ourselves, or that we are wise or good from ourselves. The combat will go on until this false idea which is signified by the prince of Persia is overthrown. And then, when the Lord has "gone forth, lo, the prince of Grecia shall come." By the "prince of Grecia," in this passage, we do not understand an antagonistic force or power. On the contrary, these words represent those who are remote from the Church, but who will receive the truths which the Lord reveals at His Second Coming. Greece has the same signification as the "isles," because of those who inhabited the islands in the Grecian Archipelago. "He shall not fail nor be discouraged, till He have set judgment in the earth: and the isles shall wait for His law." (Isa. xlii. 4.) John received a revelation from the Lord in the isle called Patmos, which was in the Ægean Sea.

The last verse of this chapter contains a promise of the New Revelation, and the teaching that those only will receive it who acknowledge the Lord in His Divine Humanity. What is said to Daniel here is said to those whom he represents, that is, those who in states of humility look to the Lord and desire to know the truth. To these He is constantly saying: "But I will tell thee that which is inscribed in the writing of truth." And of those in the heavenly societies who are especially in the love of communicating the idea that the human life of the Lord was made Divine while He was in the world, it is said: "And there is none that holdeth with Me against these, but Michael your prince." Michael, which means "like to God," represents, as before, those who are in this love and faith. "Michael and his angels fought against the dragon." (Rev. xii. 7.)

CHAPTER XI.

And as for me, in the first year of Darius the Mede, I stood up to confirm and strengthen him.

2 And now will I shew thee the truth. Behold, there shall stand up yet three kings in Persia; and the fourth shall be far richer than they all: and when he is waxed strong through his riches, he shall stir up all against the realm of Greece.
3 And a mighty king shall stand up, that shall rule with great
4 dominion, and do according to his will. And when he shall stand up, his kingdom shall be broken, and shall be divided toward the four winds of heaven; but not to his posterity, nor according to his dominion wherewith he ruled; for his kingdom shall be plucked up, even for others beside these.
5 And the king of the south shall be strong, and *one* of his princes; and he shall be strong above him, and have do-
6 minion; his dominion shall be a great dominion. And at the end of years they shall join themselves together; and the daughter of the king of the south shall come to the king of the north to make an agreement: but she shall not retain the strength of her arm; neither shall he stand, nor his arm; but she shall be given up, and they that brought her, and he that begat her, and he that strengthened her in those times.
7 But out of a shoot from her roots shall one stand up in his place, which shall come unto the army, and shall enter into the fortress of the king of the north, and shall deal against
8 them, and shall prevail: and also their gods, with their molten images, *and* with their goodly vessels of silver and of gold, shall he carry captive into Egypt; and he shall re-
9 frain some years from the king of the north. And he shall come into the realm of the king of the south, but he shall
10 return into his own land. And his sons shall war, and shall assemble a multitude of great forces, which shall come

on, and overflow, and pass through: and they shall return
11 and war, even to his fortress. And the king of the south
shall be moved with choler, and shall come forth and fight
with him, even with the king of the north: and he shall set
forth a great multitude, and the multitude shall be given into
12 his hand. And the multitude shall be lifted up, and his
heart shall be exalted: and he shall cast down tens of thou-
13 sands, but he shall not prevail. And the king of the north
shall return, and shall set forth a multitude greater than the
former; and he shall come on at the end of the times, *even
14 of* years, with a great army and with much substance. And
in those times there shall many stand up against the king of
the south: also the children of the violent among thy people shall lift themselves up to establish the vision; but they
15 shall fall. So the king of the north shall come, and cast up
a mount, and take a well fenced city: and the arms of the
south shall not withstand, neither his chosen people, neither
16 shall there be any strength to withstand. But he that cometh
against him shall do according to his own will, and none
shall stand before him: and he shall stand in the glorious
17 land, and in his hand shall be destruction. And he shall set
his face to come with the strength of his whole kingdom,
and upright ones with him; and he shall do *his pleasure:*
and he shall give him the daughter of women, to corrupt
18 her; but she shall not stand, neither be for him. After this
shall he turn his face unto the isles, and shall take many: but
a prince shall cause the reproach offered by him to cease;
yea, moreover, he shall cause his reproach to turn upon him.
19 Then he shall turn his face toward the fortresses of his own
land: but he shall stumble and fall, and shall not be found.
20 Then shall stand up in his place one that shall cause an ex-
actor to pass through the glory of the kingdom: but within
few days he shall be destroyed, neither in anger, nor in bat-

21 tle. And in his place shall stand up a contemptible person, to whom they had not given the honor of the kingdom: but he shall come in time of security, and shall obtain the king-
22 dom by flatteries. And with the arms of a flood shall they be swept away from before him, and shall be broken; yea,
23 also the prince of the covenant. And after the league made with him he shall work deceitfully: for he shall come up,
24 and shall become strong, with a small people. In time of security shall he come even upon the fattest places of the province; and he shall do that which his fathers have not done, nor his fathers' fathers; he shall scatter among them prey, and spoil, and substance: yea, he shall devise his de-
25 vices against the strong holds, even for a time. And he shall stir up his power and his courage against the king of the south with a great army; and the king of the south shall war in battle with an exceeding great and mighty army: but he shall not stand, for they shall devise devices against him.
26 Yea, they that eat of his meat shall destroy him, and his
27 army shall overflow: and many shall fall down slain. And as for both these kings, their hearts shall be to do mischief, and they shall speak lies at one table: but it shall not pros-
28 per; for yet the end shall be at the time appointed. Then shall he return into his land with great substance; and his heart *shall be* against the holy covenant; and he shall do
29 *his pleasure*, and return to his own land. At the time appointed he shall return, and come into the south; but it
30 shall not be in the latter time as it was in the former. For ships of Kittim shall come against him; therefore he shall be grieved, and shall return, and have indignation against the holy covenant, and shall do *his pleasure:* he shall even return, and have regard unto them that forsake the holy covenant.
31 And arms shall stand on his part, and they shall profane the sanctuary, even the fortress, and shall take away the con-

tinual *burnt offering*, and they shall set up the abomination
32 that maketh desolate. And such as do wickedly against the
covenant shall he pervert by flatteries: but the people that
33 know their God shall be strong, and do *exploits*. And they
that be wise among the people shall instruct many : yet
they shall fall by the sword and by flame, by captivity and
34 by spoil, *many* days. Now when they shall fall, they shall
be holpen with a little help : but many shall join themselves
35 unto them with flatteries. And some of them that be wise
shall fall, to refine them, and to purify, and to make them
white, even to the time of the end : because it is yet for the
36 time appointed. And the king shall do acccording to his
will ; and he shall exalt himself, and magnify himself above
every god, and shall speak marvellous things against the
God of gods : and he shall prosper till the indignation be
accomplished ; for that which is determined shall be done.
37 Neither shall he regard the gods of his fathers, nor the desire of women, nor regard any god : for he shall magnify
38 himself above all. But in his place shall he honor the god
of fortresses : and a god whom his fathers knew not shall he
honour with gold, and silver, and with precious stones, and
39 pleasant things. And he shall deal with the strongest fortresses by the help of a strange god ; whosoever acknowledgeth *him* he will increase with glory : and he shall cause
them to rule over many, and shall divide the land for a
40 price. And at the time of the end shall the king of the
south contend with him : and the king of the north shall
come against him like a whirlwind, with chariots, and with
horsemen, and with many ships ; and he shall enter into the
41 countries, and shall overflow and pass through. He shall
enter also into the glorious land, and many *countries* shall
be overthrown : but these shall be delivered out of his hand,
Edom, and Moab, and the chief of the children of Ammon.

42 He shall stretch forth his hand also upon the countries: and
43 the land of Egypt shall not escape. But he shall have power over the treasures of gold and of silver, and over all the precious things of Egypt: and the Libyans and the
44 Ethiopians shall be at his steps. But tidings out of the east and out of the north shall trouble him: and he shall go forth with great fury to destroy and utterly to make away
45 many. And he shall plant the tents of his palace between the sea and the glorious holy mountain; yet he shall come to his end, and none shall help him.

REFERENCES.

Verses.	Numbers.
1–4	P. P.
1 and following	A. R. 20
1 to end	A. C. 3708; A. R. 720; A. E. 31
2	A. R. 34; A. E. 50
4	A. E. 418
5	P. P.
6	P. P.
7–9	P. P.
8, 33	A. E. 811
10–12	P. P.
13–16	P. P.
13, 15, 20	A. R. 447
13, 25	A. E. 573
13, 25, 26	A. C. 3448
16, 41	A. C. 9815
16, 41, 45	A. C. 5222
17	P. P.
18–20	P. P.
21–23	P. P.
24–26	P. P.

24, 37, 38	A. C. 6075
27, 28	P. P.
27, 35, 45	Dict. P. 13
29–31	P. P.
31	A. C. 2838, 10042; A. E. 700, 1045
32–35	P. P.
35	D. Lord 4
36	A. C. 4402, 7268
36, 37	P. P.
38, 39	A. E. 717; P. P.
40	A. C. 6385; A. R. 437; A. E. 355, 514
40, 41	A. C. 2468, 3322; P. P.
41	P. P.
42, 43	A. E. 654; P. P.
43	A. C. 117, 1164, 1166, 1462; A. R. 503; A. E. 654
44, 45	P. P.
45	A. E. 405

Chapter cited A. C. 1664, 2015, 2547, 9642, 10455; H. & H. 171; A. R. 500; A. E. 734

COMMENTARY.

THE KING OF THE NORTH AND THE KING OF THE SOUTH.

The tenth, eleventh, and twelfth chapters of this book are closely connected in their spiritual sense. In fact, verses eighteen to twenty of chapter ten, seem properly to belong to the beginning of chapter eleven. The man-angel who appeared to Daniel continues to instruct him concerning the state of the Church, and to strengthen him.

Many attempts have been made by biblical scholars to explain this chapter. They have interpreted it as if it contained direct reference to the fierce struggle for supremacy between Syria and Egypt and their respective rulers, and the subsequent triumph of the Roman power over both. Antiochus Epiphanes is supposed to be meant by the fierce " King of the North," and the king of Egypt by the " King of the South." How utterly inadequate such a method of interpretation is when applied to other portions of this book, we have already endeavored to show.

If it seem to us that history and prophecy and even heavenly imagery are strangely blended in this book called Daniel, we must remember that the natural world and the spiritual world are closely related — the former exists from the latter and corresponds to it. Natural persons and things are simply used in the Word to represent and signify spiritual ideas and principles and their operation in the human mind. The church on earth is connected with the spiritual world and derives its quality from the state of that world. There is, therefore, a double representation. The scenes and objects shown to Daniel in vision were actual representations in the spiritual world, while the names of the kings and kingdoms, although derived from earthly countries, are simply used to represent the dominion of true or false principles. How they acquired their representative meanings is not always clear, but we may be sure that such representation is definite, and forms the true basis of the spiritual meaning of many portions of the Word. Such a method of interpretation may seem fanciful to some, but in reality it is that method only by which the whole Word and especially its prophecies can be seen to be Divinely inspired and full of instruction in heavenly things. "The sum of Thy Word is the truth and every one of Thy righteous judgments endureth forever." (Ps. cxix. 160.)

From verse one to four of this chapter the old dispensation, that is the Jewish Church which preceded the Christian, is again alluded to and its final destruction is predicted. We have already read of the end of the Jewish Dispensation, but prophecy is repeated in the Word. In the Word all the changing states of the churches are represented from beginning to end. The Jewish Church remained after the Christian Church began, that is, its dark shadow overhung like a cloud the spiritual horizon; just as at this day, the influence of the old dogmas still lingers in the Christian world and prevents a rapid spread of the light of the New Church. The Lord said: "This generation shall not pass away until all these things be fulfilled." The old Jewish spirit of mere obedience to the letter of the law and the idea of human authority in the Church, remains until the new generation begins, the generation of a new spirit and a new life.

The kings of Persia represent, as before, the dominion of false principles in the mind, while Grecia denotes those who are in Gentile states and have some remaining good in them. The fourth king is said to be richer than all — which denotes an increase of false ideas which finally become united with evil, then a "mighty king shall stand up." But "his kingdom shall be broken" and "divided towards the four winds of heaven." (Verses 2-4.) As the influence of Christianity prevailed the old dominion passed away, and the Jewish Church ceased to be a ruling power in the world. Thus it may be seen that although the Jewish Church came to an end as a Divine institution when the Christian Church began and the Lord executed His judgment upon the former church, yet its influence in the world lasted for some time afterwards. Even now, at the Lord's Second Coming, the Jewish spirit still lingers in the human mind, although the Jewish Church itself has long ago ceased to fulfil the purpose of its original institution.

Now, however, a new state of things is spoken of. "And the king of the south shall be strong and one of his princes; and he shall be strong above him, and have dominion; his dominion shall be a great dominion." (Verse 5.) By the "king of the south" is meant the rule or government of genuine faith in the Lord, springing from charity or love, which begins to prevail when a new church arises. As to the signification of the four quarters, north, south, east, and west, see "Heaven and Hell" 141–153, and "Divine Love and Wisdom" 119–128.

There are two principles of the Church that ought to be united, namely, faith and charity. All the divisions and troubles that have existed in the world, in Church or State, have had their origin in a separation of faith from charity, or by placing faith before charity. Faith separate from charity has already been treated of in this book under the figure of the he-goat. (Chap. viii.) Gradually the Christian Church departed from a true and living faith in the Lord which was united with charity, and degenerated into a church of creeds and forms. The "king of the north" represents the principle of faith when it begins to be regarded as the essential principle of the Church. For some time, however, there was no antagonism created between these two principles. Faith was still in some degree united with charity. It is written:

And at the end of years they shall join themselves together ; for the daughter of the king of the south shall come to the king of the north to make an agreement : but she shall not retain the strength of her arm ; neither shall he stand nor his arm ; but she shall be given up and they that brought her, and he that begat her, and he that strengthened her in those times. (Ver. 6.)

Here the "daughter of the king of the south" denotes the affection of truth remaining in the Church which seeks to be united with faith in the Lord. This affection, however, is now spoken of as degenerated; that is, it denotes the affection of truth which seeks to be joined to the idea that salvation is effected by a belief in the Lord without the works of charity. "At the end of years" refers to that state of the Christian Church when charity fell away or degenerated and the members of the Church fell into the idea of faith alone and embraced it in preference to the original doctrine taught by the Lord that charity is the essential principle. Although there were a few who still clung to this primitive doctrine of Christianity, yet they had little power and were obliged to give up or yield to the hard teaching that faith alone is saving.

From verse seven to twelve, we are instructed as to the uprising again of those who, in subsequent generations, still tried to resist and overcome the falsity of salvation by faith alone. Charity was never in fact finally extinguished; John tarried until the Lord came. All along in different parts of the Christian world, as history shows, there was a remaining love of good, which could not yield to the prevalent idea that man had no other duty than to profess a belief in Christ as an intercessor with the Father and to observe the external rites of the Church. But there were many forms of solifidianism which became so hard and strong as to resist all the gentle teachings of the Saviour of men. These two ideas could not exist together; they were antagonistic to each other and they not only produced a strife of tongues, but physical warfare and bloodshed. It was in vain that the faithful gathered their army, or that they brought the truths of the Word to overcome the false teachings of man. Reading again in the prophecy (verse 13) we learn that the "king of the north shall return and shall set forth a multitude greater than the former, and he shall come on at the end of the times *even of years* with a great army and with much substance." From this verse to the sixteenth we have a description of how the doctrine of faith alone as saving, prevails over its opposite and brings all into submission to it. In the seventeenth verse we read:

And he shall set his face to come with the strength of his whole kingdom, and upright ones with him ; and he shall do *his pleasure* and he shall give him the daughter of women to corrupt her ; but she shall not stand, neither be for him.

From this verse to the twenty-third inclusive, the prophecy treats of the changes which took place in the dogmatic theology of Protestant Christendom. The idea was introduced into the Church's teaching that charity was indeed an important principle, but that it was derived from faith — it was not the first born. Thus the true order of spiritual development was reversed — the form was put before the essence. Faith does not produce charity. It precedes it in point of time ; but only when it is united with charity are there any good fruits — thus we see how the "daughter of women" is corrupted, according to the prophecy of this book.

We are taught that those passages of the Word by which it may be confirmed that charity is the essential principle were wrongly explained, and thus the faith which is derived from charity was destroyed, and a deceitful appearance of a heavenly union took the place of the true marriage of faith and love. (Verses 24-28; see Summary Exposition.) These continual combats between true and false ideas in the mind are little thought of at this day, but ecclesiastical history confirms these explanations of the Word of prophecy. And we further see that this apparent union between charity and faith could not last; faith alone still prevailed; the "king of the north returned to the land with great substance," and every vestige of the primitive idea was destroyed. (Verses 29-31.)

There were however a few, even after this false dogma triumphed, who still opposed the teaching of the existing church and would have revived the true doctrine, but they were overpowered by numbers and wealth. (Verses 32-35.) These verses seem to refer particularly to those who still read the Word and understood its meaning, and who secretly maintained private worship and kept copies of the Word hidden from their oppressors. But at length "faith alone prevailed, a religion which destroys all fear of God and the whole Church." (Verses 36, 37.) It is very clear that this ruling dogma, which was so strongly contended for in the sixteenth and seventeenth centuries of the Christian era, hardened men's hearts to such a degree that they began to regard their own power in maintaining and enforcing it as something greater than the doctrine itself, or than any doctrine; so they worshipped themselves and honored themselves instead of honoring and worshipping the Lord. This is the "strange god" that is spoken of in verses 38, 39.

Thus it was that genuine faith in the Lord derived from a love for heavenly things was wholly subjugated at the end of the Church. (Verses 40, 41.) But there were some who escaped this destructive influence. Those who were in simple good and had little care about doctrines or knowledge concerning them, but who observed the external forms of worship, are signified by "Edom and Moab and the chief of the children of Ammon." These escaped from the hand of the king of the north. (See A. C. 3322.) There was no part of the Church nor any degree of the human mind that was not affected by this blighting influence. Even those who would know the laws of natural science and investigate the mysteries of nature became mere reasoners and lost the power of rational thinking on spiritual subjects or natural phenomena. (Verses 42, 43.) This was a state of bondage to the Church which must be broken. The concluding verses are:

But tidings out of the East and out of the North shall trouble him: therefore he shall go forth with great fury to destroy, and utterly to make away many. And he shall plant the tents of his palace between the sea and the glorious holy mountain; yet he shall come to his end, and none shall help him.

In the last state of the Church its false devotees foresee the coming judgment and endeavor to establish their doctrines in the minds of those who can see nothing beyond the sensual appearances of truth in the natural world. The last judgment was executed in the world of spirits, and it was in that world that the Solifidians built up imaginary heavens in high places, which were a "holy mountain" to them, but on either side were the false imaginations and conceits derived from merely sensual thought. These are denoted by the seas in verse 45.

These habitations in the world of spirits of those who were in faith alone, were cast down and scattered at the last judgment, which is described by Swedenborg. (See the work entitled *Continuation of the Last Judgment*, sect. 14–31.) Thus the prophecy was fulfilled: "He shall come to his end, and none shall help him."

CHAPTER XII.

And at that time shall Michael stand up, the great prince which standeth for the children of thy people: and there shall be a time of trouble, such as never was since there was a nation even to that same time: and at that time thy people shall be delivered, every one that shall be found 2 written in the book. And many of them that sleep in the dust of the earth shall awake, some to everlasting life, and 3 some to shame and everlasting contempt. And they that be wise shall shine as the brightness of the firmament; and they that turn many to righteousness as the stars for ever 4 and ever. But thou, O Daniel, shut up the words, and seal the book, even to the time of the end: many shall run to and fro, and knowledge shall be increased.

5 Then I Daniel looked, and, behold, there stood other two, the one on the brink of the river on this side, and the other 6 on the brink of the river on that side. And one said to the man clothed in linen, which was above the waters of the river, How long shall it be to the end of these wonders? 7 And I heard the man clothed in linen, which was above the waters of the river, when he held up his right hand and his left hand unto heaven, and sware by him that liveth for ever that it shall be for a time, times, and an half; and when they have made an end of breaking in pieces the power of 8 the holy people, all these things shall be finished. And I heard, but I understood not: then said I, O my lord, what 9 shall be the issue of these things? And he said, Go thy way, Daniel: for the words are shut up and sealed till the 10 time of the end. Many shall purify themselves, and make themselves white, and be refined; but the wicked shall do wickedly; and none of the wicked shall understand: but 11 they that be wise shall understand. And from the time that

the continual *burnt offering* shall be taken away, and the abomination that maketh desolate set up, there shall be a
12 thousand two hundred and ninety days. Blessed is he that waiteth, and cometh to the thousand three hundred and five
13 and thirty days. But go thou thy way till the end be: for thou shalt rest, and shalt stand in thy lot, at the end of the days.

REFERENCES.

Verses.	Numbers.
1	A. C. 1664, 8620, 10505; D. Lord 4; A. R. 256, 548, 704; T. C. R. 652; A. E. 199, 222, 717; P. P.; Dict. P. 13
1, 2	A. C. 8018
2	A. C. 10248
2, 3	P. P.
3	A. C. 2531, 7988, 8313, 9192, 9263, 10331; H. & H. 346, 518; A. R. 51; T. C. R. 606; A. E. 72; Dict. P. 13
4	T. C. R. 788; P. P.
4, 9, 11, 13	D. Lord 4
4, 9, 13	Dict. P. 13
5–7	P. P.
6, 7	A. E. 951; Dict. P. 50
7	A. C. 7051; A. R. 562; A. E. 608, 610, 761
7, 9	A. R. 478
7, 11	Dict. P. 13
8, 9	P. P.
9	Coronis 5
9, 10	A. R. 948
10	P. P.
10–12	A. C. 5376
11	A. C. 2838, 10042; A. E. 700
11–13	P. P.
Chapter cited	H. & H. 171; A. R. 500

COMMENTARY.

THE END OF PROPHECY.

This final chapter of the Book of Daniel may be said to contain the end of prophecy ; it tells of the end of the old and the beginning of the new — a state when there is a passing away of old things, and, in consequence, fear and uncertainty, and the coming in of a new dispensation when there is joy that the light has come.

And at that time shall Michael stand up, the great prince which standeth for the children of thy people ; and there shall be a time of trouble, such as never was since there was a nation even to that same time ; and at that time thy people shall be delivered, every one that shall be found written in the book. (Ver. 1.)

The words, "And at that time," serve to show the immediate connection between this first verse and verse forty-five of the preceding chapter. The "king of the south" has triumphed over the "king of the north," and the glorious reign of peace has begun.

"Michael, the prince," as already explained, stands for a heavenly society, and those who are in the acknowledgment of the Lord in His Divine Humanity. Figuratively speaking, it is always "Michael, the prince" who stands up for the Lord's people, that is, the inward acknowledgment of the Divine Human in the Lord sustains and supports the man of the church in all times of trouble. Daniel himself was sustained by the presence of angels, as the Lord was in His temptation. And in every spiritual conflict through which the Church has passed, it is the power of the Divine Truth as it is manifested in humanity that saves the world. There is always a "time of trouble" at the end or consummation of a church, "men's hearts failing them for fear, and for looking after those things which are coming on the earth." (LUKE xxi. 6.)

In regard to the spiritual fulfilment of the prophecies of Daniel since the Lord's first coming, we have indicated in our explanation of previous chapters that this fulfilment has already begun. The last judgment spoken of in the twenty-fifth chapter of the Gospel of Matthew, and in the symbolic language of the Apocalypse, has been effected in the world of spirits into which man enters after death. The first Christian Church was fully consummated at the time of that judgment. Before, during, and after that judgment, the Lord began to make His second advent through a revelation to men on earth of the spiritual meaning of the Word, and after the lapse of time a New Church began to be formed and established, in which the Lord alone was worshipped in His Divine Humanity. This new revelation, made through the instrumentality of a man, is received at this day by only a few. It cannot be proved to be true by any external evidence. The "signs" that are spoken of in the twenty-fourth chapter of Matthew — the darkening of the sun, the turning of the moon into blood, and the falling of the stars — are to be interpreted according to the language of correspondences and not naturally or literally. We do not expect to see the Lord coming in the natural clouds, but we know that He has already begun to manifest Himself in the spiritual meaning of His own Divine Word, the letter of which is as a cloud that veils the inner glory; and we know also that a time of desolation has come upon the church. The Word of the Lord is being more and more rejected by many, at the same time that a few are receiving the light of its heavenly meaning as unfolded in the doctrines of the New Church.

In the language of Daniel, "there shall be a time of trouble, such as never was since there was a nation even to that same time." This is like the language of MATT. xxiv:

For there shall be great tribulation, such as was not from the beginning of the world to this time, nor ever shall be.

These passages refer, more particularly, to the time of the Last Judgment, which took place in the middle of the last century. But the effects of that judgment are still seen; the "old" is still passing away. The conflict of faith has not yet ended on earth, because the old ideas of religion and dogmas of faith still linger in the minds of many, while, on the other hand, the light is dawning upon the minds of others.

"And at that time," it is said, "thy people shall be delivered, every one that shall be found written in the book." By the book here is meant man's book of life. In REV. iii. 5, we read:

He that overcometh, the same shall be clothed in white raiment; and I will not blot out his name out of the book of life, but I will confess his name before my Father and before his angels.

To be written in the "Lamb's book of life" is to have

the truths of heaven inscribed upon the heart. Man comes into a heavenly state of life when the truth inscribed upon the book of memory is confirmed by acts of repentance, and by heartfelt obedience to the Divine law, and is thus brought into life.

And many of them that sleep in the dust of the earth shall awake, some to everlasting life, and some to shame and everlasting contempt. (Ver. 2.)

This passage has been used as a proof of the resurrection of the natural body at the time of the Last Judgment, and of a belief in a resurrection having existed among the Babylonians or in the time of Daniel. The latter is probably true. It is stated by good authorities:

The belief of the Babylonians and Assyrians in the existence and immortality of the soul, in resurrection, in a future life, in heaven and hell is no longer disputed. The tablets found in Babylonia show this.

But this belief in a resurrection must have been very different from the true idea of the resurrection of man in a spiritual form at the time of the death of the material body which is now made known to us. Those old nations had natural ideas of spiritual realities. The latter had faded out, but the former remained. And these natural ideas served as types or images of the spiritual or heavenly. "To sleep in the dust of the earth" is a figurative expression to denote a low, natural, and sensual state of life, from which man is awakened by the voice of truth speaking to his inner consciousness, and not by the sound of a trumpet in the air.

Mankind is now awakening in part from this state of sleep. "Many," it is said, not all, "shall awake." This spiritual awakening is similar to that of a man who awakens from the sleep of death and comes into conscious life in the other world. Not all awake to righteousness, but some to "everlasting shame and contempt." And so in regard to verse three:

And they that be wise shall shine as the brightness of the firmament; and they that turn many to righteousness, as the stars forever and ever.

Those who have been obedient to the truth and have acquired wisdom from the Lord come into heavenly societies after death, and shine as the "brightness of the firmament," and those who teach others and lead them to good, shine "as the stars forever and ever." The coming of the Lord on earth was made known by the shining of the Star in the East.

But thou, O Daniel, shut up the words, and seal the book even to the time of the end; many shall run to and fro and knowledge shall be increased. (Ver. 4.)

The words of prophecy, especially of this book and of the Book of Revelation called the Apocalypse, have been shut up or concealed from the understanding of men in the first Christian Church; that is, their true, spiritual meaning was not made known or revealed before the Lord's second coming, because the world was not prepared to receive it until the church was fully consummated, until the old things had somewhat passed away, and until a separation had been made between the wheat and the chaff and the sheep and the goats. And even now, after the lapse of more than a century from the time of the Last Judgment, there are many who are kept in states of ignorance as to the spiritual meaning of the Word and the future state of life, lest they should profane what is holy. But on the other hand many are seeking the light and are filled with an eager desire to acquire new truths about the Lord and salvation. This eager seeking after knowledge, this "panting" for the "brooks of water" is denoted by the words, "many shall run to and fro and knowledge shall be increased." On the one hand there is obscurity and perplexity, a rejection of the old creeds and an unwillingness to believe that the Sacred Scriptures are a Divine revelation; while, on the other hand, there is a constant approach to the true idea of the Lord as the God of heaven and earth, and an opening of the human mind for the reception of the light of the spiritual meaning of the Word of the Lord. The Lord hides the truth and seals up the book only that it may, in due time, when there is a full preparation, be revealed unto the innocent in heart, who are called "babes" in the Gospel.

Then I, Daniel, looked and, behold, there stood other two, the one on this side of the brink of the river, and the other on that side of the brink of the river. And one said to the man clothed in linen, which was above the waters of the river, How long shall it be to the end of these wonders? And I heard the man clothed in linen, which was above the waters of the river, when he held up his right hand and his left hand unto heaven, and sware by Him that liveth forever, that it shall be for a time, times and a half; and when they have made an end of breaking in pieces the power of the holy people, all these things shall be finished. (Ver. 5-7.)

Here we have a renewal of the vision mentioned in chapter ten. A certain man, clothed in linen, appears to Daniel by the bank of the River Hiddekel. These things are said with reference to the consummation of the church. The one who inquires of the man clothed in linen, represents those who seek to know from the Lord the state of the church. There are two classes of men spoken of as existing in the church at its consummation. These are represented by the one standing on this side of the brink of the river, and by the other standing on that side of the brink of the river.

The river denotes the stream of Divine Truth which proceeds from the Lord, and thus the Word itself. The man clothed in linen is seen standing upon the waters. Those who approach the Word with the desire of knowing the truth that they may bring it into life receive the light, while those who seek it solely for the sake of themselves, that they may have honor or gain, dwell only on the natural side of truth and do not understand the spiritual meaning of the signs and wonders that are spoken of in the Word concerning the church and its consummation. The spiritual meaning of this book of Daniel, with its wonderful visions, would have remained sealed up unless the Lord had revealed it. The same may be said of the Apocalypse from beginning to end. The Word itself contains the evidence of the truth of all prophecy. What is said to be confirmed by an oath by the man clothed in linen, is spoken of those things which are contained in the Word concerning the Consummation of the Age, or the end of the church, the Last Judgment, and the Second Coming of the Lord. These events are actually revealed in the Word, but their spiritual fulfilment could not be known until the spiritual meaning of the Word was unfolded by the Lord. This was made known to Daniel, for we read:

And I heard but I understood not; then said I, O my Lord, what shall be the issue of these things. And He said, Go thy way, Daniel; for the words are shut up and sealed till the time of the end. (Ver. 8, 9.)

In regard to the expression "time, times, and a half," they simply denote a fulness of state, or a full consummation which must come before the Lord will make His second advent. In the book of Revelation, the woman, who symbolizes the church, is said to "fly into the wilderness where she is nourished for a time, times, and half a time from the face of the serpent." Here the spiritual meaning is the same as that in Daniel.

In explanation of this passage in REV. xii. 14, we read:

It is of the Lord's Divine Providence that the church should at first be among a few, and should increase gradually among many, because the falsities of the former church must first be removed, as truths cannot before be received; for the truths which are received and implanted before falsities are removed, do not remain and are also dissipated by the dragonists. The case was the same with the Christian Church, that it increased gradually from a few to many. (A. R. 547.)

Many shall purify themselves and make themselves white and be refined; but the wicked shall do wickedly; and none of the wicked shall understand; but the wise shall understand. (Ver. 10.)

We may compare this with REV. xxii. 11:

He that is unjust let him be unjust still; and he that is filthy let him be filthy still; and he that is righteous let him be righteous still; and he that is holy let him be holy still.

At the time of the Last Judgment, and in the judgment which awaits every one after death, those who are in evils and have confirmed themselves in them remain in them. It is not the Lord's pleasure that this should be so, that is, that the wicked should remain in evil after death, but it cannot be otherwise, since the Lord cannot change evil into good nor destroy the freedom of the human will.

And from the time that the continual *burnt offering* shall be taken away and the abomination that maketh desolate set up, shall be a thousand two hundred and ninety days. Blessed is he that waiteth and cometh to the thousand three hundred and five and thirty days. But go thou thy way till the end be, for thou shalt rest, and stand in thy lot at the end of the days. (Ver. 11–13.)

We have before shown in explaining these prophetic sayings that the numbers of days, weeks, or years have no reference to natural time but to states of the church. The "daily burnt offering" refers to the representative worship of the Jewish Church which was abolished when the Lord came into the world. Then a new state arose. But the "abomination of desolation" refers to the end or consummation of the first Christian Church.

The time from the Lord's first coming to the Last

Judgment embraced the whole period of the duration of the first Christian Church. So long as any remains of good were left in that church men were saved and entered heaven, but for the most part those who entered the heavenly societies from the Christian world during that period, especially the latter part of it, were infants, who had not, of course, profaned any truth or adulterated any good. From these the " new heaven " could be formed. As there were many who waited for the " consolation of Israel " at the time of the Lord's first coming, so there were some at the end of the first Christian Church who waited for their Lord. These receive the glad tidings of His Second Coming. They are called " blessed," because they cherish a firm belief that the Lord will come, although they know not the day of His coming. But when the spiritual meaning of the Word is revealed to them they rejoice in the light. The final injunction to Daniel is the Lord's injunction to all His faithful followers; for Daniel in this verse represents those who wait patiently and believe in the Lord.

" Go thy way till the end be," means that every one must walk in the light and live according to it until the judgment comes. Every one finds his place after death either with the evil or the good, according to his life in the world. The Psalmist declares:

The rod of the wicked shall not rest upon the lot of the righteous; lest the righteous put forth their hand unto iniquity. (cxxv. 3.)

This doctrine of the New Jerusalem, that man should

live according to the Lord's commandments, faithfully doing his part in the great drama of life, is written throughout the whole Word in history and prophecy. Peace and blessedness come not from merely thinking or believing, but from loving and doing.

The crowning glory of the New Church, signified by the New Jerusalem, will be a perfected humanity, developed in order from the lowest degrees of life to the highest — man created and recreated, renewed, regenerated, and disenthralled, an image and likeness of the Glorified One who appeared to Prophets and Apostles and Who has called His people out of the bondage of Egypt and the captivity of Babylon into the light and freedom of the Holy City.

INDEX.

	PAGE
Ahasuerus	95
Ancient of Days	117–119
Antiochus Epiphanes	6
Astrologers	39
Astyages	95
Babylon, Capture of	90
Beasts, Four, Vision of	114–117
Belshazzar	81, 82
Belteshazzar	21
Book of Daniel	1–13
" " " Apocryphal additions to,	12
Chaldeans	18–41
Churches, Most Ancient, Ancient, Jewish, Christian, New-Jerusalem,	42–47
Cyrus	7, 31, 154, 155
Daniel	13–20 et passim
Darius the Mede	7, 95
Dreams	111, 112
Ecclesiastical History	47
End of Prophecy	181
Feast of Belshazzar	83
Fiery Furnace	60–63
Gabriel	19, 132
Grecia	163
Hiddekel	159, 187
Horn, Little	130
Horns, Four	130
Image, Great	43
Inquisition, The	99
Jehoiakim	23
Jehoiachin, or Jechoniah	24
Jeremiah	140, 141
Josephus on Daniel	14
Jewish Church	145
King of the North and King of the South,	172–177
Kings, Four	120

	PAGE
Kings of Media and Persia	90, 133
Kings of Persia	161, 172
Last Judgment	148, 150, 189
Lycanthropy	70
Magicians	39
Man Clothed in Linen	157, 158, 187
Mene, Mene, Tekel, Upharsin	88, 89
Michael	19
Nebuchadnezzar	23–26
Necho	24
New Jerusalem	17, 191
Numbers	142–144
Prayer of Daniel	102
Profanation	84, 85
Ram and He-Goat	126–128
Raphael	19
Resurrection	184
Roman Catholic Religion	54–56
Sacrifice, Daily	131
Satraps	97
Shadrach, Meshach, and Abednego	55, 59–63
Sheep	126, 127
Shinar, Land of	5
Shushan	125
Son of Man	118
Son of the Gods	62
Song of the Three Hebrew Children	61
Sorcery	40
Tarshish	158
Tigris	159
Tree, Nebuchadnezzar's Dream of	71–73
Vessels, the Sacred	27, 85
Wars	126
Winds, Four	113
Wine	83, 84
Writing on the Wall	86
Zedekiah	14

www.ingramcontent.com/pod-product-compliance
Lightning Source LLC
Chambersburg PA
CBHW020239170426
43202CB00008B/152